STORIES MAKE PEOPLE

Examples of
Theological Work in Community

Compiled by Sam Amirtham

WCC Publications, Geneva

Cover design: Rob Lucas

ISBN 2-8254-0963-4

Printed in Switzerland

Table of contents

Introduction

People need theology, it is often said. All Christians need a right understanding of their faith, for the sake of right belief, right worship and right living. People need theology to live by; they need theology to give account of the hope in them. The task of the theologians and scholars is to provide such theology that all people can appropriate.

But it is equally true that theology needs people. For the sake of vitality and faithfulness, for the sake of relevance and wholeness, theology needs the experience and faith reflections of all believers. It is they who live amidst the conflicts and challenges of everyday life, it is they who strive to relate their struggles and aspirations to the faith. The believing, worshipping and practising people of God have something vital to contribute to theology. The theological task of the church cannot be left to the scholars alone; everybody needs to be a subject and participant in this enterprise. This is a new concept, a relatively new conviction.

When people become participants in doing theology, theology must take other shapes than that of systematic treatises. People will then create new and appropriate forms. For people not only enrich the content and perspectives of theology, but also diversify the forms and shapes of theology. Among prevalent forms of people's theology are "stories", narratives, dramas, conversations, group discussions, personal musing, Bible reflections, and also songs, poems, drawings, paintings, etc.

So we say, people make stories. This itself is a revolutionary concept. For it has always been held that "story-tellers" create stories. People only listen to them. The stories give them certain roles in life and places in society which they often passively accept. Some stories lull them into a conformity, others challenge them and arouse a new awareness. Whenever the latter happens, people begin to construct and reconstruct their own stories. For in telling new stories, or old stories in a new way, they rewrite, remake their own history. By telling Bible stories differently, and by making new faith stories, Christians are creating a new identity, and indeed a new church.

Stories indeed make people, in this sense. When they begin to tell their own stories of God acting in their daily lives and in the lives of their communities, they do so from their own perspective and out of their own conviction. Then faith becomes a living faith, a lived-out faith. It restores to them the dignity that belongs to those made in God's image. As they speak to God in prayer and speak about God in theology, they affirm themselves as God's children.

The Programme on Theological Education (PTE) has been promoting the concept of theology by the people, on the one hand encouraging communitarian ways of doing theology, and on the other hand inviting people involved in formal theological education programmes to listen to this new form of theological activity and respond creatively to them. The Mexico letter to colleagues in theological education said:

> As we consider our task as theological educators, we are humbled before God and before God's people. We now see more clearly that we must learn to listen to the stories of suffering people as they tell of their hope and work for justice in the midst of oppression. We need to learn their language, interpret their experiences and stories for ourselves and others in the light of the gospel, and make available to them the experience of the universal church, the wisdom of the Christian tradition, and appropriate critical tools.
>
> We need to learn to read the Bible not only with the tools of scholarship but also through the eyes of the poor and the marginalized, in order to understand God's message and make our response as disciples of Jesus Christ. We need to be changed in accordance with this understanding.

In fact, when Christians gather together to do theology in community, often it is around the Bible to study and reflect on it in new ways. In this process, the scriptures are being rediscovered and reappropriated as a source of life and faith in a challengingly relevant way. Some of the contributions in this volume are examples of this.

An earlier volume (*Theology by the People*, WCC, Geneva, 1986) carried reflections by scholars *on* doing theology in community. This volume, as suggested by the PTE Commission and the WCC Central Committee, is an attempt to collect actual stories of people doing theology.

As it will be seen, this new phenomenon of "theology by the people" — a new movement of the Spirit, we believe — is not confined to any one part of the world. We have stories here from Asia, Africa, Europe, Latin

America and North America. Some of them are group stories — narrative descriptions of what really happened in groups; others are personal stories — the reflection of one person; and yet others stories of stories — reflections on the stories. The very fact that most of the contributions are written by more than one person is itself significant.

The concern has been not only to show how these stories express fresh theological and biblical perspectives, and how they are shaped in new forms, but also to indicate how new patterns of training for ministry are emerging. It is a call for theology and ministry, as well as theological education and ministerial formation, to be in community.

The underlying conviction is that the whole people of God are the primary agents of the basic theological and ministerial vocation of the church. Every believer has a role to play and every one is invited to do so.

Stories Make People

DON CARRINGTON and JOHNATHON HOGARTH

This article is an account of an actual workshop with Aboriginal community development workers and church leaders. A group of twenty-one delegates from eight different Aboriginal communities in Northern Australia camped together for a week in June 1987 to begin a process of conscientization and community development.

These particular people and communities had been subjected to many different community development projects over the years. Overall, no real progress was being made. Projects and educational efforts thus far had weakened the people rather than empowering them.

The workshop was conceived using alternative methodologies and the apparent foolishness of stories in an effort to open the way for the empowerment of Aboriginal leaders, in and of themselves. Rather than resorting to imported community development solutions, the faculty aimed to facilitate perceptions appropriate to Aboriginal struggles from the delegates themselves.

Biblical and cultural stories were used as catalysts in a process of affirming self-worth with participants who had been the "objects" of many development projects over the years. In our evaluation, the workshop did in fact succeed in facilitating a "developmental paradigm shift" such that the people present at the seminars did begin to grasp their new role as "subjects" in control of their own history. In engaging with stories told by facilitators and in sharing their own stories they caught a vision of tribal Aboriginal people actively engaging in self-development projects. Some in fact gained the confidence to become theologians in their own communities.

Perhaps a significant feature of the dynamics of this seminar was that faculty present, particularly those academics with doctoral qualifications, set the tone by telling liberative stories about "frogs" and "asses" and thereby signalled that it was "OK" for participants to tell their stories in whatever terms they wished.

Session One: Two short stories by way of introduction

The coordinator began: "Firstly, let me tell you a story of a community of frogs who lived at the bottom of a deep well. This story first came to my notice in a book by Rubem Alves entitled *What is Religion*. These are not exactly the same words as used by Alves, but the story goes something like this:

At a place not too far away from here was a deep dark well, where for a very long time a community of frogs had lived. The well was so deep that none of them had ever visited the world outside. They were convinced that the universe was the size of their well. And what is more it appeared to them that there was more than enough scientific evidence to support this theory and only some mad frogs who were to be pitied would say anything different.

It happened however that a small bird flew by one day and saw the well, became curious and flew down inside. How surprised he was to discover the community of frogs! The frogs on the other hand were even more puzzled and perplexed by this strange feathery creature who called in question all the age-old truths held by their society.

The bird could not have pitied them more. How could frogs live their whole lives trapped in that well without at least the hope of being able to get out? It was clear to this little bird that the idea of leaving the well was absurdly foolish to the frogs because if this hole were the universe then there could be no "out there". So the little bird started singing furiously. He trilled of the soft breeze, the green fields, the leafy trees, the crystalline rivers, butterflies, flowers, clouds, stars — which put the frog society in a flurry and the frogs became divided. Some believed the little bird and began to imagine what it was like to live out there. They croaked new songs. The others frowned. "Such stories unconfirmed by our own experience ought not to be worthy of our faith. The little bird must be singing senseless lies." And they began to make their philosophical, sociological and psychological criticism of the bird's songs. Whose cause was this bird serving? The dominant classes? The dominated classes? Was this song something of a narcotic? Was the bird crazy? Who knows, it might be a crazy dream? There was no doubt that this song and this bird were creating many problems.

Neither the dominant frogs nor the dominated frogs (who were secretly preparing a revolution) liked the ideas which the little bird was putting into people's minds. So they planned and waited and on his next visit the little bird was imprisoned, accused of being a deceiver of the people, killed, stuffed, and all the frogs were forever prohibited from croaking the songs the bird had taught them.

"Secondly, I want to remind you of the story of Jesus with the blind man at Bethsaida (Mark 8:22ff.). This blind man was touched twice by Jesus. The first time he saw people but they appeared to be trees walking around. He could not see clearly. The second time Jesus touched him he saw people not as trees but as they really were. He saw people clearly."

Two points were illustrated as the story was told. Firstly, that Jesus used ordinary earth and saliva to perform this healing, and secondly that this is a story of blindness and then of rapidly improving sight. This gives us hope as we begin to seek insights into our communities that we shall be able to discover clarity of vision.

Session Two

At this point the participants broke into community groups and were given chart paper and pens and asked to report back with a picture that reflected the story of their community. Participants were told that the story may be personal or communal in nature. And at this point another of the faculty present, who was himself an Aboriginal person, told a story of the conversion of a drunkard and of the community of which he was a part. One option that people were given was that they "map" their community and in speaking about the map tell their story.

The following three reports are representative of the people's first efforts.

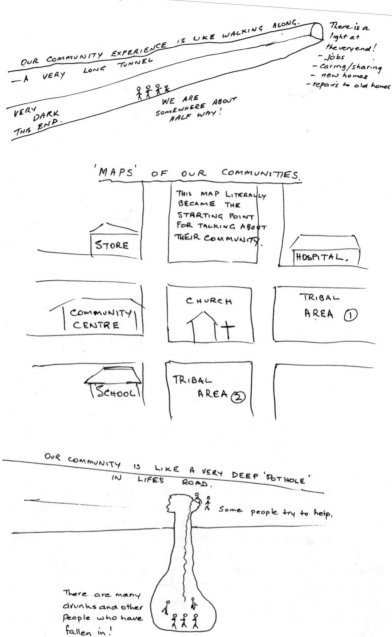

Session Three

In the evening of the first day we concluded with a Bible study entitled, "Hope for People in the Brickyard". This story was based on the first chapters of the book of Exodus and the account of life in the brickyard owes much to the work of W. Brueggeman and his book *Living Toward a Vision*.

The Exodus story was retold, with faculty giving detailed input regarding the emergence of hope for the people who were enslaved. From a situation of oppression in Egypt the people cry out. God hears their cry and God takes action. Moses is sent to Pharaoh with the challenging message: "Let my people go!"

The ensuing battle of wits between Pharaoh's sorcerers and Moses culminates with a real power transfer. When the magicians could no longer imitate Moses hope is born. The emphasis at the end of this first day is therefore that after Moses utters the words "Let my people go!" in the brickyards of Egypt everything changes. When those words are uttered the world is no longer a hopeless place.

The small groups discussed this story briefly and people went to bed expressing the thought that "God did it once and he can/will do it again".

Session Four

The biblical story which we considered at the opening of our second day's work together was that of Balaam's ass recorded in the book of Numbers 22:22. The story was retold with vivid detail as the participants were basically rural people who understood horses and their behaviour. Attention was again drawn to the need for clarity of vision. That people really need to see what is going on around them. In the Balaam story there was danger ahead and he couldn't see it. By contrast his donkey could see what he couldn't see. The story was left open-ended as a precursor to the day that was before us.

The remainder of this session was led by a visiting lecturer who dealt with a "felt-needs approach to community development". Needs are like an iceberg in water if you break off the top they surface again. There are basically three types of needs in the community: those you see; those the people see; those both see; The comment was made that it is of little value to work with needs that you alone see. People in the community have various needs and it is better to start with those a group sees. People grow through working together.

Session Five

At this time the groups once more continued to share stories and pictures from their communities.

After one mapping exercise, participants who, it was stressed, were the experts regarding their reality, said in a rather depressed way: "We can't see anything good out of it" (i.e., the situation and township in which they were living). The big expressed need was for a hall for youth activities. But the comment was also made: "We are really lost." (It should be noted that this is not an uncommon initial response from tribal people who have become urban fringe dwellers.)

Spontaneously at the end of this session the Aboriginal faculty person who was sharing in team leadership rose and referred once again to the Balaam story. In a humorous way he stood on a chair and said: "I am that ass." He then went on to say: "Let me tell you what I see.

"I see the 'white church' as being like the curtain fig trees found in those regions. These trees begin to grow by seeds being dropped in the branches of an existing tree where they germinate and send down long roots, sometimes twenty feet into the soil far below. Many missionaries come to sit in the branches and to send down their long roots like snakes into the ground. These roots eventually kill the native tree (and turning to the remaining faculty group he remarked 'You white fellahs will disagree'). But I reckon that the original tree is the original traditional Aboriginal faith in God and a strong tall tree is the community stuctured on that faith. The tree trying to grow from the top down is the big problem."

Offering an alternative picture he then asked that the seeds that they planted as Aboriginal community workers should grow from the ground up and not from the top down like a curtain fig tree.

"White people said come up to us rather than them coming down to us." "They made us jump up." Our Aboriginal God was named Yirrmbal. Our faith was rooted in the soil and was a strong tree. People had not seen this God "Yirrmbal" but they looked to him for protection for life and for hunting. He was understood as the creator of all.

Then the church came and said "Get rid of that God" and come up to ours — rather than saying that we could know Yirrmbal in Jesus Christ. Hence the resentment of the missionaries. Aboriginal faith in God has been cut off and perhaps only 5 percent of Aboriginal people have been able to make the leap from tradition to faith in Jesus.

This seminar is to discover a new way of seeing and communicating so that you will realize that you are just as equipped as any European to see and talk with God. If you are going to keep going the European way, you are going to have problems, especially those who come from community backgrounds. Maybe we need to go back to our stories and our language.

Some Aboriginals put culture against Jesus. But Jesus came into Jewish culture, enriched and transformed that culture. He did not come into European culture first. Don't say that Jesus does not fit into our culture or know our stories. He gave them to us and they often resemble biblical stories.

This faculty person then went on to say: "Culture is the guide-line for communication. Your people are equipped to communicate the gospel more than people who come in from the outside."

Session Six

Groups were then given time to enhance their first drawings in the light of these new sessions. In addition they were asked to "sketch out the sort of Aboriginal church they would build in their community".

One group reported back: "My drawing is different today because the tree has been chopped down." This comment evoked much laughter.

In this sketching of his community and the church the reporter mentioned the primary ceremony of the area called "Bora". He mentioned an insight from a book written by David Thompson, called *Bora is Like Church*.

Bora is a very big thing to us and it was good to discover that it was like church. Now we realize that God did not give us the Bora for nothing and we must use it. The group notes the tribal rivalry of the four main tribes. In the light of the previous speakers' comments this local group resolve amongst themselves to "Try to grow the seed from the bottom up with God's help".

Many other groups responded reflecting their own struggles. In summary, another group reported as follows:

> How thankful we are for culture. For camp-fire meals of Aboriginal food. For our stories (here two traditional stories were linked with Bible passages).
> We like the possibility mentioned of speaking, singing and making music in traditional languages. Faith and prayer are doorways to change.

Again spontaneously a woman commented with much emotion: "This is the best meeting I have ever been to. We have never been given an opportunity to share these things ourselves."

At this point our Aboriginal staff person confessed that he was glad that he had stirred up a hornets' nest and that he believed that they had begun to respect their tribal identity again, including their traditional language.

Session Seven

Opening a new day's work together, we began by looking at the narrative of the first few months of Jesus' ministry. This series of stories carried the subtitle "Jesus and the Birth of Hope for Galileans". For a short time we looked at a map of the people and developmental struggles in Jerusalem and Galilee. We tried to appreciate that Jesus was led by the Holy Spirit into Galilee which was a place of mixed races of people experiencing rejection and discrimination. "These were bush people and the proud people of Jerusalem looked down on them." In the eyes of the religious people Jesus worked with "rabble who knew nothing of the Law".

Jesus seeks John's baptism and God is pleased. He is on the right track. But Jesus does not stay camped out by Jordan. He is tempted to enter different styles of ministry but after the time in the wilderness he moves to Galilee and into the rabble area. His first sermon in his home town takes up Isaiah 61 and speaks of hope for the poor.

At this point our Aboriginal staff member again explained that as the result of the last two days' work the agenda had been changed. People were already making connections realizing that the risen Jesus takes the lead into Aboriginal "Galilee" communities. His additional recapitulation of the previous day's point was to stress again that the task was to find ways of communicating within cultural structures rather than expecting people to drift into a church to hear the message.

Groups were formed to redraw some of the maps with this aim in view.

One community drew a most innovative picture of their vision of the church.

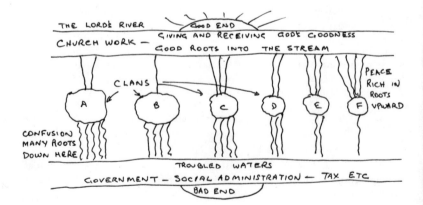

After this presentation our Aboriginal faculty person quipped: "I feel like packing up and going home." The response from the Aboriginal presenter of this group report was: "OK, I can take over."

Session Eight

The concluding biblical story for that day was of the healing at the pool at Bethzatha (John 5). This story was dramatically retold and enacted. We noted that this healing took place on the Sabbath when people did not expect any stirring of the water because angels rest on the Sabbath.

Jesus comes from a completely unexpected direction from over the hill behind the people (back door) at a time when people do not expect miracles, and asks the man lying there if he wants to be made well. We raised the question as to ways in which people become comfortable in their paralysis. The implication of Jesus' encounter with this man is that his healing is within him and Jesus calls for a faith response.

One listener said: "Our churches may be like that pool. Our faith should not be in some miracle occasionally in the pool, but in the people whom Jesus calls. We need to see where Jesus is working, and this is 'from behind' not from in the pool." The day closed with the whole group discussing their own reflections on each other's stories in the light of Jesus' action calling for faith and healing.

Session Nine

On the fourth day, the work was opened with the story of Moses and Jethro from Exodus 18.

The old man Jethro sees Moses overburdened with work and concludes that Moses is "not doing things in the right way". His advice to Moses is to share the work and to organize for more participation.

Some creative comments made during the discussion of this story included:
— "Jethro is not of Moses' faith and maybe is in a sense like some of our traditional elders who have tribal wisdom."
— Maybe we should do some Holy Spirit inspired dreaming about the words of Jethro: "You are not getting this development business right…"
— What action words come up from our pictures and who can share in the action for development?

One group showed a significant difference to previous thoughts. Their new plan of action was:

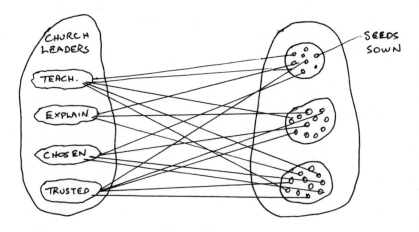

This contrasted with what was termed the old model:

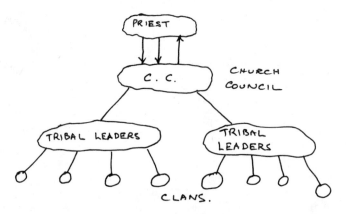

Their conclusion was that we need each clan group to do some teaching through their chosen representatives. The old model, participants concluded, tells me that I should not be involved.

While this active group work was taking place, our Aboriginal faculty person had been making his own creative connections. In plenary he summarized how far we had come, by referring once again to the oppression in Egypt and to Moses. Then he said: "Looking at the diagrams you have all drawn the message is clear:
— we are oppressed;
— we are nobody;

— things are not done in the right way; they are unjust;
— we do not know what to do;
— nobody is listening;
— nobody is understanding;
— there is nobody to talk or to share with;
— nobody to share our troubles with;
— nobody seems to care.

It all boils down to oppression, frustration and injustice.

I am trying to get you to forget that you have been told how to do things by whites. And what about our church councils? When I challenged the make-up of our church council I was opposed. The whites did not like the names I chose because they saw that some of them were illiterate people. But these people did the job well.

The white way is to have authority on top but the Aboriginal way is to have people on top. We need to look at clan authority structures in order to bring more people into our fellowships. One great Aboriginal value is that God put it in us to look after our own people. This way we can see that God works through the people from the grass roots up. Not as a bird coming into the branches from a long way off.

Session Ten

This session opened with a creative exploration of different interpretations of Bible stories where diversity is part of God's plan. The question was asked, was the Babel story in Genesis 12 a story of blessing or a story of a curse?

The story-teller wants us to believe that there was a time when everyone spoke the same language. However this assertion by one story-teller does not agree with the actual situation reflected in earlier chapters of Genesis. After the flood the sons of Noah and their families speak different languages. The group looked at Genesis 10:20ff. It appears that it is the strong desire of the Babylonian story-teller that all people speak one language and build a tower in Babylon. Thus the perspective of this story is to impose one dominant language and one culture by forced labour. God's creative action was to destroy the town and to create diversity of peoples. To want one language is forcefully to apply the philosophy of assimilation.

The biblical story-telling now leapt forward in history to the Pentecost experience and made the observation that the Holy Spirit spoke through a diversity of languages and not that all heard the one language. The witness therefore of Pentecost being further evidence of God's use and initiatives in a diversity of languages and peoples.

Theologically the group consensus was that God inculturated himself in every language and culture after the Ascension and the coming of the Holy Spirit at Pentecost. "So getting to express yourselves in your own culture and language is just what the Holy Spirit wanted."

The coordinator then moved to Peter's cultural conversion and the story of Cornelius in Acts 10. The essence of our look at this story was to observe the struggle of Peter who was a Jew and thus a member of a culture and people who taught that God favoured their Jewish culture. When Peter sees the Holy Spirit fall on the Gentiles he has a cultural conversion. What God has sanctified no one may call unclean.

Session Eleven

The opening session of this final day was given over almost entirely to Aboriginal myths and stories, the group coming to the profound conclusion that the Aboriginal Dreaming with its inspirations and as it is manifested in symbols and stories can immeasurably enrich Australian Christianity.

The participants were then asked: "Which stories have you found the most significant this week?" One lady answered: "The story of the frogs down the well. Also the story of the bird in the branch and the need of the church to grow not from the top down but from the bottom up. We know that some frogs go brown in the dry climate when they are not fed well. We are just like those frogs, unless we share the faith and teaching as we are doing here we will dry out and go brown."

Person after person replied: "The picture of the frogs down the well." Another said: "People are only thinking of the well. They are not thinking of anything outside their own communities." Various people had commented about Jesus and the bird. Willy, the present speaker, continued: "Some people have taken Jesus and stuffed him by their images and ornaments of the cross, etc. These people have no idea that the bird came down into the well for a purpose. I am encouraged by this seminar because I find that some frogs elsewhere do have a vision."

Another man remarked: "While we were here we got some very good teaching to take home, especially the teaching from Willy and Jerry" (please note that neither of these were faculty). This comment led others to mention the contribution of faculty and their contribution was summed up in a spontaneous sentence which characterized the whole experience. "I am sure that the Holy Spirit was quite happy to use the faculty to help us to discover ourselves."

A brief analysis of this "workshop" experience

The educational philosophy underlying these initiatives towards the empowering of Aboriginal community leaders is based on narrative and praxis approaches to community development and to doing theology. The method requires that a seminar or workshop begin by catalyzing an agenda from the leaders and people who are the participants.

This methodology is necessarily life-based, problem-centred or alternatively a situational model of curriculum development actively evolving by cooperative planning between faculty and participants.

Much preparation takes place before the event, but often much of this planning has to be revised, sometimes scrapped, because in the final analysis this kind of seminar cannot be pre-planned. The agenda shifts as people grow.

Two prerequisites were present. Firstly, Aboriginal people work with a holistic philosophy of community development in which it is impossible to separate religion/theology from community development. Secondly, maximum flexibility is required in order that faculty might be responsive to developments during the course of the week. The exercise was government funded and subject to certain parameters. In response to education department requirements the daily timetable was as follows;

1) sharing our stories of people's development from our own country;
2) talking together about some community development stories from overseas;
3) mapping community development stories from the Cape York region;
4) talking about "our maps" of our communities.

Thus context-specific life stories were basically the evocative guides in the project proposal. The rest of the week's activities grew out of this daily schedule creating a constant dialectic oscillating between discovering new dimensions of community experience and the further recreation of the pictures "mapping" factors and forces at work in their home communities.

Faculty to work with such a methodology need to trust people; to insist that the people do in fact have the ability to do theology and are able to change their world as co-creators with the God of freedom.

In relation to the Bible and theology the starting point for reflection is the life of the people, not scripture per se or doctrine. Theology becomes the second act. <u>Bible stories become open-ended invitations to explore further</u>. The educators' role is thus to enter into dialogue with people about concrete community situations and to offer the people instruments with which they can make their own discoveries.

Part of the educational presuppositions underlying this methodology has been a careful study of Jesus' use of parables. Parables demand a creative theological and educational response from those who listen. Parables empower people. When Jesus interacts with his hearers, time and again we noticed that "in parables" he invites people to participate in a creative way and at the same time avoids open conflict. In parables he succeeds in a remarkable way to: (1) continue to retain the initiative; (2) avoid compromise of his position; (3) allow the story to "speak compassionately" in so far as when as teacher he tells a story it often has a challenging yet "hidden" meaning. Jesus requires an initiative of appropriation on the part of the listener as to whether "the point" will be understood or not...

The Aboriginal people of Australia as far as possible relate to one another in a non-confrontative story fashion. When an Aboriginal person wishes to give guidance to another person this must be done indirectly so as to avoid impoliteness and confrontation. More often than not, the way a person who wishes to speak "strong words" must proceed is to tell a story which talks in an indirect way in the "third person" about situations removed from any present potential conflict. A biblical example of this technique in communication was Nathan's challenge to King David.

Faculty had observed that often in conversation with tribal people, a story will be told which seems totally unrelated to anything past or present. Almost in frustration one wonders: "Why on earth did that person tell me that story? Was he or she trying to tell me something important?" If the listener cares enough to ponder deeply the story and the complex inter-relationships concerned, the message and burden of the story may emerge. Stories of this nature keep open the possibility for reunion and reconciliation rather than challenge in aggressive ways which makes open conflict inevitable. Stories speak gently of matters which if conveyed directly would send the spears flying.

A particular characteristic of Jesus' teaching in some of the most volatile explosive situations is the way what he says is not forced on people but is rather compassionately offered for those who have ears to hear. Stories invite people into community development activities at points where they are willing to participate.

A key point was reached on the second day when our only Aboriginal faculty member spontaneously rose to play "Balaam's ass". His exposure revealed two points. Firstly, that in many parts of North Australia the externally imposed church has imposed its European structure and authority. This has strangled the traditional Aboriginal faith in God which has had no room for expression, integrated as it is with social structures and Aboriginal law.

This led him to his second emphasis. If a truly Aboriginal Christianity is to be recreated then the delegates need to realize their own culture and its expressions are a prime resource.

> This seminar is to teach a new way of communicating, maybe, but you need to realize that you are just as equipped as any European to see this God. If you keep going the European way you are going to have problems, especially those who come from community backgrounds. Maybe we need to go back to our own stories, myths and legends.

This was a radical thesis and hence the donkey role freely taken by the speaker. Its strength educationally lay in its compatibility with the narrative approach already begun. The delegates were led to believe in their own resources and not just to get some new facts from the seminar. This realization led to a marked upturn in creativity by the delegates; thus even on the second day the success of the methodology could be clearly seen.

Evaluating the stories which were seen as most noteworthy, 85 percent of respondents mentioned the frog story. This is hardly a coincidence. It had been simmering for a whole week. Now it encapsulated the deepest felt paradox of their identity. A way that was felt to be credible had been shown to the Aboriginal delegates to get out of the well. Its very credibility made them feel more intensely their predicament and strive more creatively with means of escape. These discoveries are the very currency of conscientization and the empowerment of people.

Onesimus: a New Outlook on Family

JANE HAAPISEVA and JENNY BERLIE

Where we live, in the Swiss countryside near the city of Geneva, the most penetrating outreach or Christian service of the local Protestant church has been the formation of neighbourhood groups where many people (especially young women) who are not otherwise involved in church activities come into contact with biblical texts. A well-known biblicist and talented Bible study leader, U. Rüegg, leads a session with the local group leaders, who then repeat the same exercise in their own neighbourhood group. Thus prepared to give some background information so that participants will understand the text better, the "leader" has also ready a method of approach, such as miming or drawing, and an overall view of the aim of the discussion and application of the text. Each local meeting takes place in a different home and the leader is supposed to change each time (although that is not often the case).

We feel that our group is particularly vital and enjoyable. Mrs Treboux is a countrywoman whose children have grown up. Her husband still farms the land. She has a lovely garden and orchard. Mrs Frei's husband is retired. They moved to the village many years ago. Her daughter-in-law, Domi, lives under the same roof with her teacher-husband, several children and pets. She has recently opened a centre for homeopathy for which she is much appreciated. Margaret and her husband are Swiss-German. Her three young boys are sometimes very trying for her. Yvette and her husband run the village post office and have both grown up in the area. Heidi, originally Austrian, and her Swiss husband have lived in Montreal, New York and Australia. Twelve years ago, they settled down in a large farmhouse in the middle of the village. She is an artist and active Sunday school teacher. Régine and her husband are German. They have bought a pretty home in a row of neat, small, new and expensive houses typical of the region. Dominique is a young farmer's wife who has worked as a psychology counsellor for young single women in the city. Kristina is the wife of a Swiss doctor. She teaches handicrafts in the local schools and is on the church council. Christine, who has Indonesian and Dutch blood, is enthusiastic and refined. She lives in a house near the golf course, an ancient monastery, somewhat at a distance from the rest of the village. Monica is a young mother. She grew up in California, but had Swiss parents. Linda also. She has a diploma in medicine from the University of Geneva, but is at present mothering four small children. Jenny, though Swiss, spent many childhood years in Turkey where her parents still live. She and her husband are gradually taking over his family dairy farm. Theirs, along with Dominique's, is one of the old families of the region, which live three generations together. Jenny appreciates broader contacts. She, Linda, Domi, Margaret and Christine are Catholic. Jane is from Canada, has been involved in church life since childhood and has completed theological studies in Brussels and in Geneva.

Of the fourteen of us, perhaps only four or five have husbands who would willingly participate in a Bible-based discussion. About the same number attend church regularly or occasionally. Sometimes, one wonders where exactly is the church here; one feels that it is in these ten or twelve groups which meet five times a winter. Here people's thought patterns are opened and expanded about the character of Jesus and his mission and about God and our relationship to God. One hears less and less questioning about the existence of God and more and more about the manner in which the church and its clergy carry on their mandate to worship. Those of us who have already long ago or more recently lost interest in the formal, Sunday morning worship in a three-quarters' empty church accept gladly an invitation to one another's living room to be questioned and to think things through anew.

Our theme has been "A new outlook". The last meeting focused on Jesus' attitude towards his relatives in Mark 3:31-35, which led us to a new outlook on the *family*. Jesus considered all those his brothers and sisters who were "inside", sitting around him and learning from him. This evening we again consider the family, or the home, in *Paul's letter to Philemon*. It's Jenny's turn to lead. We read Paul's letter together and Jenny presents the members of Philemon's household.

Jenny: Philemon is the owner of a small industry, perhaps of textiles. He is a Christian and a friend of Paul. Apphia is his wife, and Archippus, a brother or close friend who has also been a working companion of Paul in spreading the Gospel. Then there is a community, a church, that meets in Philemon's home and it is made up of his slaves and some from other establishments and free men and women. Onesimus is a slave who has run away from Philemon. His name, "Profitable", which would have been given to him by Philemon when he bought him, is a bit ironic, since it sounds as if Onesimus has been responsible for some money transaction that has turned out to be a financial loss to Philemon. Now Onesimus has found protection in the person of Paul and has even become a Christian and valuable co-worker himself to Paul. Paul is sending him back to Philemon with this letter of recommendation.

Christine: One sees that Philemon is placed in a very difficult situation. Should he pardon Onesimus and accept him back into his household?

Margaret: Paul's asking for more than that: he's suggesting that Philemon should receive Onesimus as a brother, as if Paul himself were Onesimus. What will the reaction be of the rest of the household? Especially of the other slaves? Won't this look like favouritism?

Linda: But Philemon will have to do something, because Paul himself may, in fact, be dropping in soon.

Heidi: Paul's letter is phrased in such a way, we can see he wants to obtain something from Philemon. He praises him and his goodness so that Philemon could hardly refuse to do the good thing Paul's asking of him. Maybe Philemon was not exactly the example of love that Paul makes him out to be.

Dominique: Paul does not refer to Philemon's attitude towards his inferiors and slaves, but to his loving actions in the church community. It's two different things.

Jane: But the one should extend into the other.

Jenny: What would we recommend as a solution to this situation if we were Philemon, or Apphia, or the church in their home?

...silence...

Kristina: It's almost impossible for us to say, since our own homes are so different. We can't easily put this in a modern setting.

Jenny: Here's a drawing that shows us what the Roman conception of a household was. Basically, it was a system that maintained *order*. Everybody had his or her place and was content in it. (she explains the drawing)

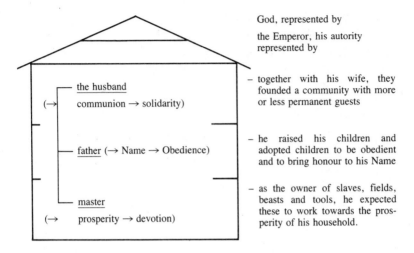

God, represented by

the Emperor, his autority
represented by

– together with his wife, they
founded a community with more
or less permanent guests

the husband

(→   communion → solidarity)

– he raised his children and
adopted children to be obedient
and to bring honour to his Name

father (→ Name → Obedience)

– as the owner of slaves, fields,
beasts and tools, he expected
these to work towards the prosperity of his household.

master

(→   prosperity → devotion)

Yvette: It looks as though Philemon could have adopted Onesimus.

Jane: I think when a slave reached a certain age his master could free him so that he could marry, even though he would still stay in the household.

Heidi: Philemon will keep Onesimus as a slave, but their deeper relationship will have changed.

Yvette: Even if it's a change in their "deeper relationship", won't it still be difficult to maintain the "order" that Jennny talked about?

Dominique: For Apphia, it would be a change, if she should lose a good slave.

Margaret: She should uphold her husband's decision. No, I mean she should quietly influence him to make the more loving decision. And the church there is going to be a buffer between Philemon and Onesimus. They should both urge Philemon to pardon him.

Jenny: If you were Onesimus, how would you see your new place and role in Philemon's house and community?

Régine: Onesimus should continue to serve humbly and even better than before his pardon and reintegration.

Christine: I would think he would be tempted to be haughty and to feel himself elevated.

Linda: If Onesimus looked after financial business, he must have had some education, so he could understand what Paul had taught him about liberty and pardon from the point of view of a slave.

Jane: It's true that in the New Testament, we often find the notion of the slave-master relationship used to express Christian attitudes.

Linda: I mean that Onesimus was probably not just any slave. He might have been taught by Philemon himself. They may have grown up together. So the disappointment and reactions after his running away would have been all the more violent and Paul's sending him back as a Christian and a co-labourer in the church all the more impressive.

Dominique: By the way, it looks as though Paul really had enough of his own money if he was ready to reimburse personally any loss to Philemon.

Linda: That shows that Paul really had "adopted" Onesimus in the family way, since he was even ready to pay his debts.

Jane: That brings us back to Paul's words to Philemon, that he, as an authority in the church community, had the perfect right to command Philemon to behave in such and such a way to Onesimus. But he already there set the example of not using his authority and instead, expecting an act of love.

Régine: If Paul expects an act of love from Philemon, then Philemon should probably expect continued obedience from Onesimus, whether he adopts him as a son or not.

Linda: No. He will be just as devoted, but his obedience will be different. And if he is taken back as more than a slave, then his share in the prosperity of the household will be different.

Jenny: What do you think happens, according to Paul, in a Roman household when Christ enters the picture?

Kristina: If Philemon's household is "Christian", now when Onesimus comes back there must be some upsetting in the usual order.

Jane: Christ always brings change and an opening of possibilities.

Jenny: Yes. It is no longer a hierarchy. God is no longer at the top. The place of the emperor has been filled by the crucified Christ.

Jane: That's right! In the last study, we saw that Christ's brothers and sisters were *around* him. Now God is in the centre in the person of the crucified Christ.

Kristina: ... who came not to be served but to serve. Paul did not command Philemon but urged him on in a loving way.

Yvette: But is it possible to be a loving father or brother and a boss at the same time? Can someone who has to, for example, fire an employee show brotherly love? We know of a Christian man in that circumstance who ended up committing suicide, rather than fire a lot of his employees when that seemed to be the only solution to the financial problems of his company.

...silence...

Kristina: It's not only the relationship between the employees and the boss of a household that must change. It's also that of the husband and wife. There should be more of a free and responsible communion between them.

Margaret: If the centre is common, that is the crucified Christ, then decision-making must be shared, financial questions resolved together, prosperity shared.

Linda: I see what you mean. Obedience in an upward direction in the hierarchy becomes solidarity between brothers and sisters.

Jane: Of course, because what has changed is the ultimate value of each person before God. The Christ has been crucified for each and for all and each has his or her own relationship to him.

Jenny: Even the slave's first allegiance is now to God. The word "communion" has become central. The slave accepts this communion which elevates him to being in solidarity with others. (she shows this on the diagram)

Finally, our last question is how should we live out brotherly and sisterly relationships in our own society. Where can we find negative and positive examples?

Christine: Well, I don't know if suicide is a negative or positive example, but from making a difficult situation, it sure got Yvette's friend off the hook!

Linda: I think the lesson is about opening up. We should get beyond our normal vision of the nuclear family. Paul wanted to see Philemon's household built up upon a foundation of love and openness instead of being the model of order and convention. The God of Jesus-Christ is not a God of order but of peace.

Dominique: Order does not always bring peace.

Christine: But peace always infers its own order.

Yvette: Our Swiss society is particularly orderly... and peaceful.

Kristina: But are we open enough?

Jane: Christianity does not do away with social structures: it transforms them. For me, the idea of us all being brothers and sisters and the opening up of the nuclear family has many implications. We are more dependent on people we would not normally consider as being part of our "family". On the other hand, we can release those who are, so that each person can be free to fulfill his or her individual personhood. We don't "own" our children and children are put in a position where they can "forgive" their parents, for instance.

Dominique: Someone said earlier that in the church, we don't choose our brothers and sisters. That's true. We choose our friends in society, but it's only when we think of ourselves as brothers and sisters that we have real solidarity and are able to share in the prosperity of the life in the community.

The Cross Bearers

SELVANAYAGAM ISRAEL and ESTHER RETNARAJ

This is of course a single voice, but it is also collective in a sense. This will become clear in the course of my story,[1] a story mainly based on my autobiography but it relates to many other biographies in a "spiritual" manner. In that sense it is a heterobiography. At the first instance it may not look like a community reflection. Yet I believe it points out what is authentically community in my own context which is typical of the Indian context at large.

My name is Priya, literally "dear one". I am a housewife; my husband is a clerk in the city corporation office. We lead a simple family life in Madurai, a city known for numerous temples and wayside shrines. Meenakshi, the fish-eyed goddess, is the presiding deity of Madurai. Though I could only study up to the school final, intellectually I am sharper than my husband according to people. When my parents arranged my marriage they did not consider whether we "matched" intellectually — or in any other way. My husband is a devout Christian; I too am a Christian, but we seldom go to church together because my husband's tradition is "high church", whereas I am from a congregational back-ground. He is the cross-bearer in the choir, and very proud of this role.

Once I heard his pastor praising him for his performance as cross-bearer, taking solemn steps, holding the cross reverently. In addition, I myself have been a cross to him, as he would say often.

As a traditional Indian woman I had kept my dark secret for a long time. But it came out one day, when I heard a moving sermon by a guest preacher at a Sunday service. He was preaching on Revelations 13:8, on the symbol of a lamb slain from the foundation of the world. He said God, who is in Christ, has solidarity with those who are perpetually battered —

---

[1] This is based on the story of a member of the congregation of which Esther is a member.

the slaves, women and children in India. His description of the many-sided sufferings of women in our society was powerful. He said: "In many bridal marches in wedding services what I see is an innocent lamb, i.e. the bride, being led by her own guardian to a slaughter house; she never opens her mouth (see Isa. 53:7; Acts 8:32). It is true that she is adorned in fine clothes and much gold, and is greeted by many. But all such delights remind me of a sacrificial lamb brought into a shrine on a festival day nibbling the festoon leaves happily before the fatal blow. So also are many women in our society; Christian women are no exception." Hearing this I burst into tears, giving vent to an emotion hidden for a long time. It brought me closer to some of my friends in the church and our neighbourhood. But it only hardened the heart of my master, my husband.

My husband often abuses me. If I protest, he hits me. What he says is final. I have no right to contradict him. It is all biblical, according to him. I have never dared to expose his image of himself. Should not a wife be the glory of her husband, as St Paul says?

We do not have children. We have been longing for one. According to the doctor I can bear children. But my husband is not willing to go for a medical examination. He won't let me talk about it. I suggested long back that we adopt a child from an orphanage but he won't hear of it. He thinks in biblical terms and is convinced that I am barren, by which he is cursed. Once, advised by a sectarian preacher, he talked to me of Sarah, Hannah and Elizabeth who were deeply distressed and wept bitterly before the Lord and got children. Nothing is impossible for God; therefore, following the example of these great women of the Bible I should cry before the Lord. He has many sectarian preachers as friends. There is no way I can tell them of the damage they inflict upon people like me with their pseudo-spirituality and superficial understanding of the Bible.

The prestige of a man depends on the humble submission of his wife, so say the great teachers of India. I am sufficiently brainwashed to take this literally. But the contradictions and tensions involved in this position are sometimes unbearable. I have to serve food and eat the left-overs. I cannot even talk to my husband while he is eating. There were times when I would cry uncontrollably in the kitchen. But he would shout at me and ask me to lower my voice and suppress my sighs. I have become a great actress in a tragic drama at home. If a guest comes to the house unexpectedly I am expected to stop my crying, wipe off the tears and smile. I have tried pleading with him, but he won't relent. All he wants is uncritical obedience. If I go against this unwritten law, he would ask:

"Have I bound you or have you bound me?" The *tali*, the wedding chain he tied around my neck at our wedding, as a sign of "constant faith and abiding love" according to the CSI wedding service, is for him, like for most Christian husbands, a noose around the neck, a binding force. I must respect this noose although sometimes I feel like throwing it in his face. With a similar sense of obligation, I have to submit to him in bed.

Don't you think that such a woman, who has nobody at home, not even a child, needs some fellowship to share her problems and pray together? Yes, we have an active women's fellowship in our church. We meet every Sunday evening. Our pastor's wife is its president and another "soft and nice" woman is its secretary. But at every meeting we hear nothing but the stereotyped slogans of obedience to husbands on all occasions, following the footsteps of the great women of the Bible. Beware of the so-called disobedient women of the Bible! No corporate discussion and reflection. Breaking the tradition, once a member of our women's fellowship, who later became a close friend of mine, tried to share her sufferings at the hands of her in-laws because she didn't bring a big dowry. The immediate response from the chair was: "Don't bring personal and family issues here; we are here for prayer and fellowship; such things we must put up with." My friend kept quiet. But we had a detailed sharing after the formal meeting was over on the steps of our church. This type of informal sharing grew week by week and a few more joined us. Such meetings, not liked by the pillars of our church and not known by our husbands, helped us greatly because we could unburden ourselves. However, we do not want to give the impression that a counter-fellowship is being organized against our church women's fellowship. We know most of the problems we have are applicable to Indian women in general and our religious traditions seem to perpetuate oppression on the basis of scriptural authority. Once my friend pointed out to me that the passage usually read at functions of giving the dowry money to the groom and his parents (so she had heard from a woman theological student) is from Genesis 24 in which it is said that gifts of gold and silver were given to the bride and her parents and not the other way round! How ridiculous it is to read this passage when the man is the recipient! Poor pastors, they know not what they do!

The pervasive influence of a progressive seminary situated in Madurai needs due acknowledgment. It is a source of encouragement for women like me. Guest preachers are invited from this seminary and a group of students come regularly to help our Sunday school and youth fellowship. They always touch upon the key issues in the common life of our society.

For this they have been often criticized by the custodians of the church traditions. Wife-beating is a cowardly and inhuman act, one preacher from this seminary boldly said once.

Once a team from the seminary organized a seminar in our church in which some problems of women were thrashed out. It was in the context of considering the question of women's ordination for the first time in our diocese. Usual objections were raised but the way in which things were clarified was very enlightening. One important topic in this seminar was the proper interpretation of the Bible by placing different passages side by side. St Paul, for example — it was pointed out — perhaps in a context in which the Christian women's new upsurge in public gatherings appeared to be disturbing for many, goes to the extent of asking women to be silent. He finds support for his argument from certain passages of the Old Testament. For Paul, Adam was formed first, then only Eve, and Adam was not deceived but the woman was deceived and she became the source of human transgressions. Man is the image and glory of God but woman is the glory of man. Man is not created for woman but the vice versa (1 Tim. 2:13-14; 1 Cor. 11:7-9). It is interesting to note that here Paul quotes one of the two creation accounts, the second one, found in Genesis 2:1-3:7. But on the contrary Jesus quotes the first account which says that from the beginning of creation God made the human beings male and female (Mark 10:6; cf. Gen. 1:27). And Genesis 2:24 which says "therefore a man leaves his father and his mother and cleaves to his wife, and they become one flesh" is quoted by Jesus (Mark 10:8) positively over against the law for divorce, whereas it is quoted by Paul in a negative sense to indicate the sinful relationship of a man with a prostitute (1 Cor. 6:16). Besides, if we take all the passages of Paul on women together we can notice the other side of his attitude towards women. He writes, for instance, that in Christ there is no female and male (Gal. 3:28); in the Lord woman and man are interdependent and made for one another (1 Cor. 11:12,13). Here is a clue to identify passages and counter-passages within the same Bible. And also, it was said in the seminar, women are the living tools of interpretation for certain fundamental ideas of the Bible like the intercession of the Spirit with deep sighs and the groaning of creation in travail (Rom. 5:22,26). This made me realize the worth of being a woman.

I came to realize more and more that women's problem is not a Christian problem only, although I believe that the Christian gospel contains profound ideas for women's liberation. The role of mass media in creating a new awareness among women has dawned on me only very recently. A friend of mine showed me an article a few months ago from a popular Tamil journal. There a Hindu woman, who has been battered by her husband and harassed by her in-laws, says: "For the simple reason of going round the sacred fire at my wedding I have a fire bath every day." Another item in the same journal was a review of a Tamil movie. The heroine, after a long struggle, comes to a drastic decision. She buries all her scriptures and runs away. Anyway I do not have the courage of this kind nor do I find a final solution in this, I must confess. But I cannot discuss such things publicly because for many Christians including my husband reading a secular magazine or going to a movie is a sinful act.

Such awareness created by the mass media and a critical reflection of the Bible as mentioned above have certainly influenced some thinking Christians. Some recent events in our church prove this fact. On Christmas Eve the year before last the young girls of our church staged an interesting play entitled "Christmas Mother". In this play they presented the tradition of Christmas Father as another historic symbol of male domination and suggested having a Christmas Mother, something unheard of. On another occasion, a girl pointed out in a speech certain popular proverbs in the Tamil language which support women's oppression. She called for a study of enslaving proverbs for the formulation of new proverbs, liberative and enlightening.

I am sure you'll be interested to know about the response of my husband. You must have also noticed that now my concerns are not confined to myself and to my home. Since my husband loves to be the cross bearer in the choir of another church, normally he is not aware of what is going on in our church and he would never expect any change in my traditional attitudes. He is not as yet prepared to share with me those concerns. Nevertheless, I find greater meaning in life and I have some hope that his attitude will change. He has given me little opportunity to love him, but have I given God an opportunity to love me? God tells the rebellious people: "How can I give you up... my heart recoils within me, my compassion grows warm and tender" (Hos. 11:8).

If only I had a child! He/she would then be my great companion, and there could be a new atmosphere at home which in turn would change my husband's attitudes. But I should not be too hasty and I must accept the limitations of life. My mother, who lives in a village some distance away, wrote to me a few years ago: "Do not expect changes to take place in society and home with the ease and speed of rice cooked in a pressure cooker. This is a temptation for girls like you living in cities. You know, I still cook my rice in an earthen pot, and I still use firewood. That involves struggle, frustration, tears and patience. The kingdom of God does not come overnight."

Some of you may criticize me. So slow and hesitant. But that is how I am. My story, however, has not ended. What we need from you is not sympathy, but a new interpretation, an interpretation of life, of the life of many like me. Perhaps more painful than the physical pain Jesus suffered on the cross was the kind of interpretation given for his suffering by the passers-by, questioning all his authority and power. But the early church gave a different kind of interpretation for his cruel death — a loving God in solidarity with suffering humanity. Most of us women in India struggle between love and bitterness, between emotional bonds and social bondage, between inherited traits and liberative moves.

You can identify the crosses we carry in subtle forms, in words, gestures and action, interpret them, thus giving meaning and strength to us in our suffering. We need people who will continue to raise questions like: where is the community of reflection in our local congregations? Who are the subjects of our interpretation and what are our resources? Which questions do we raise? Is Jesus the answer for every problem? But you see, Jesus cannot be the answer for questions which people don't ask.

A Theological Word for Today

FRANCINE CARRILLO and FRANCOISE LARDERAZ

For this article we have decided to report on what has been done by the participants in the eighth group of the Ecumenical Theological Workshop[1] on the text of Genesis 2 and 3 (Eden and "the Fall"), as it is a narrative of which believers and unbelievers alike have some inkling. Our entire culture, indeed, rests on it and our entire anthropology has been shaped by it. The story often arouses resentment or a sense of guilt and it is always "unfinished business".

Straight away let it be said that we are working in this eighth ETW group on the theme of freedom and that this study is, more precisely, part of a sequence called "Freedom and Prohibition", in which we are trying to show that Christian liberty is not to be found in an absence of limitations but always derives from a Word that wants us to be free.

Three of us who were theologians had to prepare this presentation, and the more our reflection progressed the more we discovered that the story is not one about punishment but reveals how freedom involves risk. We have tried to share this discovery with others for, to our mind, a theological word for today can come alive only if one has been prepared to change one's own position. It can only emerge when we are taken existentially by surprise.

The work was done in two two-hourly meetings. The first took the form of a workshop (work in groups) and the second was a theological review (a lecture followed by discussion).

The workshop

Each group was helped by a theologian and an animator with exegetical notes and a programme outline (for this work we were greatly stimulated by Marie Balmary's book, *Le sacrifice interdit*,[2] in addition to the classical exegeses).

Before turning to the text itself we asked those taking part to recall for themselves the story, drawing from their memory what they knew or imagined of God, Adam, Eve and the serpent. The exercise was exciting and made it possible to see the position *from which* everyone was speaking (i.e. their personal history and the kind of religious and confessional language that had so far influenced them), and the stance from which each would be listening afresh to the Genesis story.

Here are some items from this brain-storming which revealed that memories were focused on punishment:

— Adam was made from clay, lacked courage and was stupid.
— Eve was taken from Adam's side (dependence of woman); she initiates and is the instigator.
— God: creates, is powerful, vindictive, requires obedience; gives the man and the woman freedom but also the forbidden fruit.

He walks in the Garden and speaks:

— to the woman: "in pain you will bring forth children";
— to the man: "you will toil with the sweat of your face";
— to the serpent: "upon your belly you shall go. The woman [sic][3] shall bruise your head" "and you shall bruise her [sic] heel":
— Adam and Eve are banished.

The first stage, in which the position of each participant was brought out, seemed especially crucial to us for, as we see it, theological discourse which does not take seriously the position from which people understand what is said is liable to remain no more than talk; it never becomes a meaningful Word exerting existential pressure to bring individuals to see things in a new way.

We then went stage by stage over the route traced for us by the story, starting from the idea that Genesis 2-3 is not intended to explain evil but is a narrative which is trying to think theologically. In this we were aligning ourselves with Von Rad's standpoint: in theological thinking and even more in the popular imagination, ideas about what relates to "humanity's first state" and "the Fall" raise more questions than they answer. Also, certain conceptions about happiness and the state of first innocence have imperceptibly infiltrated Christian thought from outside the Bible... This text will be totally misunderstood if we do not let it speak for itself.

In the text of Genesis 2-3 there are probably three narratives woven into one:

1. A narrative about the creation of man [sic][4] (2:4b-6,7-8,18-22,23-24) where before he comes on the scene he is already there *in absentia (!)*, as *something missing* at the heart of the world, something which, as it were, God the creator wants to plan (Gen. 2:4b-6).

God makes man in two complementary actions: he moulds him from the earth (from the start man is frail and mortal; in no way is he made of something that is divine) and breathes the breath of life into him (which is the sheer possibility of being a living being, i.e. capable of entering into relations). Then he puts the man in the garden (2:7f.).

But something is not right: the man is on his own (2:18). So God associates him with himself in his work. Adam classifies the animals by naming them but does not find "a helper fit for him" (2:19f.). This helper will be given him (which is the point of his "deep sleep") and this explains why he cannot control his wife's origin any more than his own (2:21f.).

And when the woman comes on the scene, the man in his astonishment speaks. When he talks about her he is talking about himself, no longer as the one made of earth [*Adamah* = earth, ground (translator's note)] but as a human being, *îsh* (masculine) vis-à-vis *ishshah*[5] /feminine) (2:23).

Verse 24 concludes this narrative. It tells of God's good design for the man and the woman. Their relation can be a live one only if it is based on a *breach* (with father and mother) and on a new *attachment* which expands beyond the couple (this may be in the shape of children, but not exclusively so).

This first text taken by itself would present a falsely optimistic picture of the creation of humanity. Moreover it is not for nothing that Eve is given her name only in 3:20.

2. A narrative describing the primordial garden (verses 9,10-14). This on its own brings us closest to the myth of "Paradise lost". Here we find the trees and their fruits. The narrative tells how it comes about that access to the tree of life, which was possible to start with, finally becomes impossible. The reason is the introduction of another tree, the tree of the knowledge of good and evil.

There is also a river with four branches. This gives us our bearings in our discourse and our world, these two cardinal points representing desire and space. The river flows out of Eden. So there is a way out of it. Eden is not a cloistered Garden of Delights under the eyes of God.

3. A narrative with a commandment for human beings, their transgression of that commandment and the bestowal by God of a new order which turns the new situation to account (2:16f., 3:1-7,8-13,14-24).

By forbidding them to eat of one tree alone, *God is preserving and guaranteeing the position of the "other" (2:16f.).* He sets a limit which allows the other to exist. The difference between the sexes is a metaphor for all the other differences. Speech — the word God utters — is the medium for the appearance of the prohibition which guarantees life, permits relationships and establishes law.

But when the word is distorted the relationship which is both right and possible (for they were both naked and unashamed in 2:25) becomes the occasion for frustration and a lack that has to be concealed (they know they are naked and make themselves "aprons", 3:7).

Distortion of the word is the work of the serpent who subtly does it, changing not the words of the commandment but their position. God had said "of every tree" (2:16) except one. That is, not every tree. But the serpent claims God had said "not... of any tree", that is of *none* (3:1).

The woman is so flustered that three mistakes slip into her reply:
1) God did not talk about fruit but about trees;
2) God did not prohibit touching:
3) the forbidden tree is not given its precise name, hence the trees are confused.

The woman turns God into someone who encloses her in a mesh of prohibitions. The prohibition is no longer seen as a single line separating two beings and preserving their freedom; it is a territory defended by a despot for him alone to enjoy (3:1-6).

But God still seeks out the man [sic]: "Where are you?" (3:9). The first time Adam says "I ..." in this narrative is to say "I was afraid, I was ashamed" and this he does as an excuse, blaming the other (the woman and God who put the woman beside him).

There is no real dialogue in this passage. Now, a truly human world is a world in which there is discourse. Hence God for his part will speak again with an "I...". He creates something new by making three ordinances through the *word* (3:14-19):

— to the serpent:

"I will put an enmity between you and the woman, between your seed and her seed": it is part of God's plan to contrive a long-term struggle between those who hold established power, which sees itself as deficient in nothing and those who only have the marks of that power branded on them, that is, for us, the stranger, the poor, the sick and the mad.

— to the woman:

"in pain you shall bring forth children... your husband... shall rule over you". She is branded in her motherhood and wifely status — the two things which (at least in that age!) constitute the deepest dimensions of her identity.

— to the man:

> "cursed is the ground because of you". The issue here is his relation to the earth, the environment and unproductive toil.

Since they were unable to maintain the difference between them, the man and the woman find themselves back on their own, *like one isolated element of a relationship* — which is as far removed as possible from "being (like) God" (3:5) since for his part God is otherness and otherness is his image.

But God does not abandon his plan. In 3:20 Eve is called "the living one", the "mother of all living". So life is possible right in the midst of banishment and fragility and God preserves it with infinite tenderness, for he makes himself responsible for providing clothing for the man and the woman (3:21).

What is given in Eden is certainly what is right for us but the lesson of the story is that this happiness remains illusory and a delusion if we do not risk living here and now in history. That is where ethical decisions have to be taken and where our freedom and creativity are exercised. Because of them, in a word, the Paradise of which the Bible speaks is less the country from which we have come and to which we would have to return than *the land of promise for us.*

At the end of the workshop we asked some of those taking part to share their reactions with us. Here are some comments which testify to what was discovered:

Genesis 2 describes God's plan for humanity which inevitably has not been experienced by us. Genesis 3 describes our life.

The man in 2:21 sleeps. He does not know where his wife comes from any more than he knows his own origin.

The wife is taken from the man's rib-cage: the rib is also the side, the limit where "the other" can begin.

The man receives the woman as a gift (2:22).

The woman gives the man identity. Through her he affirms himself in communication and exists. The reverse is also true!

The prohibition is placed before the creation of Eve to show that "the other's" place must be preserved.

The Eden situation can be rediscovered only if otherness is respected.

The tree is rather the "tree of choice" than the "tree of knowledge".

God's plan for humanity is not a past that has gone for ever but something lasting and for the future.

As I left the workshop I realized that I had never liked this text; I felt it was violent, that it created guilt and devalued... so I had set it aside and kept Genesis 1 and 2 in my mind. The workshop made it possible for me to discover this Bible passage and to *like* it. Above all I noted the term "God's plan".

The theological review

In the second meeting, after a quick indication of how Genesis 2 and 3 functioned in Judaism and Christianity as a means of justifying woman's inferiority, we offered the participants a translation by A. Chouraqui to make them notice the hazards of translation, which are likewise those of interpretation. Comparison with the French ecumenical translation of the Bible made it possible to bring out something new and come to terms with certain words which till then had been given a negative connotation.

In a report given by two of us, we then took up some points likely to contribute to our reflection on "Freedom and Prohibition". We deliberately said the same things, but differently, to make the material provided more easily digestible.

— The narrative does not tell of a punishment but reveals the risk freedom involves

The account of the "beginning" in Genesis 2:3 is a product, not itself a beginning: what comes first is the life of a people which recognized the face of the God who liberates in the work achieved in its history. However at the time when the narrative was given its shape (tenth century B.C.), when the Davidic empire was at its height, violence was still distorting human relations, the law of the covenant was often flouted and war might break out any moment. That was when the prophetic voice emerged and addressed a question *to all human freedom*: "Israel, where are you?" (cf. Gen. 3:9). On which ground do you stand? In the name of which God are you living?

Israel then tries not to explain evil but to think it out theologically, on the one hand avowing that the liberating God is also the Creator of a good creation and on the other that the disruption of that good creation rests on humanity's transgression of an invisible but extremely real limit.

But the acknowledgment of that "disobedience" appears in the narrative like the reverse side of a promise and a goodness subsisting beyond the disobedience. The creator God is also the re-creating God, as the saga of the patriarchs was to narrate later on, beyond the Deluge and the Tower of Babel. The promise is at work all the time to transform humanity's exile into a new domain where they truly could dwell and try to live what is the most impossible life-style, yet what is exhibited here as the norm: a single humanity in the image of God, made of two beings at once different and equal.

The text of Genesis 2-3 tells of how human beings relate to God, their fellow-creatures and their environment. In the structure of their human relations, human beings find the marks and evidences of their relationship to God. In the narrative there is no question either of original sin or a Fall; reflection is not aimed at relations which are interrupted and then restored, but on a situation of dream or reality.

— A Word which sets bounds and makes it possible for the other to exist

The situation of reality is marked by the setting of bounds: human beings are creatures limited by a Word of command, a "programme", and by a domain which by definition involves a missing element — a lack; they are never a whole; they come under a constitutive delimitative ordinance; and do not themselves register the true gauge of good or evil, happiness and unhappiness. The narrative of the beginning defines the conditions for life as a reality and not *the* reality of a life to which there should be a return after leaving the garden.

The Word of God and the serpent's word are structured on the theme of the missing element, the *every* and the *not every*; placed in the garden by God, humans have a knowledge marked by restriction because of the Word. God's "not every (tree)" shows that there can be no identification with the environment: if there were nothing that could not be eaten humanity would be in danger of taking over the whole of its environment. It would be in danger of confusing itself with the whole... Now in this whole God establishes missing elements or gaps: he operates by *exclusions* which are the mark of the *presence of the Other*: it is the function of the trees that cannot be eaten to be reminders of the Word of God. Such exclusions also mark the presence of *the other*: the woman taken out of the man is a reminder of what he lacks: and as she is regarded as an "other" by the man this makes it impossible for her to fill the lacuna; the woman does not fill the gap in his rib-cage; she is not the supplementary element which would make it possible to make one out of two... the androgyne cannot be reconstituted. The woman remains *other*. She is also a reminder of the relationship to God since it is he who effected the extraction.

— Discourse which leads humanity to deny the difference

The contradiction between God's commandment and what the serpent says in distorting the grasp on reality is structured on the "not every (tree)". The serpent presents God as humanity's rival and commends a state of perfection in which human beings would — immediately — dwell in a kind of unlimited wholeness because of the "every". The serpent drives the man and the woman to identify themselves with the environment by appropriating it.

Thus there are two ways of looking at the "not every": as a lack that can be interpreted as the *mark of God* who specified what the trees were; or as what can still be eaten. This second way represents *desire* and *imagination*; the first is *symbolism* (with trees which by not being available and by their separation operate as reminders of the Word, and structure humanity's relationship to that Word). This also produces two ways of looking at God: is he a *God who speaks* or a *God who knows and sees everything?* From the "tree of knowledge" we have the "sees everything": to know everything is to see everything: so the man and the woman realize they are naked. By covering themselves they try to deny the differentiation and go back towards wholeness, neutralizing what is the fundamental difference in humanity. They hide the sign of the radical lack to which effect was given while he slept. And they also go backwards by representing themselves as trees: no longer are there a man and a woman in the garden.

— A freedom experienced in distance and in the "missing element"

God reaffirms the need for the "not every" by insisting on the nature of the distance and of the lack: the woman is going to lack even more than the man: she is given a specific role: she is responsible for history. This establishment of woman as subject or initiatrix is signalled by distance from the man; but in her body she rediscovers traces of the "not every": the problem of suffering, of the bruised heel and of the irksome handling of her relations with the man. Men and women note that it is *possible to suffer because of the lack*: we speak of domination and desire, etc. Men remain bound to the soil but because of the irksomeness just described, the environment displays *otherness*: the soil resists providing freely things to eat; the metaphor of distance is conveyed by the need to work the soil. And of course man is *in time*, which is a factor of delimitation and finitude. The temporality within which future generations are confined becomes a symbol for the "not every".

This condition of humanity therefore involves risk: those elements set up as signs of God's otherness are also elements on the basis of which desire can be turned into covetousness. Thus what the serpent says is always possible because it is written into the structure of things. But by closing the Garden to humanity God shows that there must be no dreaming: humanity must become involved in its history knowing that it will always be marked by the elements of lack and limitation.

— *A freedom between the two trees*

In the story there are two trees (which may have belonged to different traditions). Both are in the midst of the Garden, together indicating life and limitation. Here the limitation is that by which existence is sustained in truth, that which the story leads us to believe is really *the place of the other*.

The point of the tree of life is to indicate that creation is a blessing. It says that man and woman can be alive. The tree of the knowledge of good and evil (= to know everything and be able to do anything) is the tree of choice, offered to everyone in their freedom. It indicates that it is possible for human beings not to receive but to refuse the gift. God took a risk when he created human beings — the risk of evil and atheism. With the bringing together of the two trees in the same narrative it is possible to show theologically that human beings are created good but that it is in their nature to fall short. In this sense their being forbidden the tree of knowledge stands as a sign of promise, for it witnesses to the fact that God's will is to protect them against themselves.

— *A Word to tend*

The classical interpretation of the prohibition is that it preserves the otherness of God, not because God is jealous of his prerogatives (it is the serpent's work to suggest that) but because humanity could not put itself in God's place without destroying the work of creation.

Now, in the narrative, the prohibition about the tree of knowledge comes *between the creation of the man and the creation of the woman* and this means that here God wants first and foremost to ensure that the position of "the other" is respected. The tree of knowledge establishes otherness not in the first instance between God and humanity but between the man and the woman, for that is where God is really to be found. The Hebrew helps us to understand:

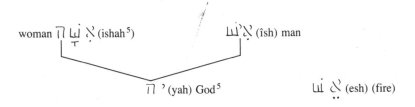

If the man and the woman are able to pool what makes them different, they find God. If they put together what is like in both of them they are but a devouring fire.

So "the other" is not for "eating" — for "consumption" — but for communication, on the basis of the first Word spoken by God, establishing a complementary relationship of opposites for man and woman.

What, when all is said, is to be worked at in this garden, where everything seems to grow by itself? One thing only: the Word ordained by God. "Ordain" here is not "command" with a view to obedience. It implies rather the setting forth of a Word which creates order for "the other" to exist. If the word is to gain a hearing the distinction between the creatures must be preserved.

In God's intention the woman is "a helper fit for"[7] the man (Gen. 2:20). The person who said that knew a bit about marriage! Woman is at man's side and communicates with him but she is (over) against him if the communicating word stops circulating between them.

Making full use of the Word preserves it from the threat of the serpent for whom sight is more real than speech, since what the serpent says is "your eyes will be opened". Seduction stakes everything on sight (3:6) whereas from the biblical standpoint seeing starts with hearing. I am alive if I place myself where the word is, the word which indicates for me where "the other" is. When I depart from that way and then only consider the other as "a delight to the eyes" (3:6) death is all that remains.

These are our freedom stakes and they are to be played for in the precariousness of our existence, where God himself constantly seeks us — "Where are you?" (3:9) so that he can bring us to where communication occurs.

The discussion that followed brought a wealth of assent and dissent. We sum it up in the words of one of the participants, a psychiatrist:

> It is hard to swallow the bit in Genesis 2-3 which talks about transgression and punishment. Our whole unconscious speaks to us in terms of guilt. And inside myself there is often a note of accusation: "how can God allow that?"
>
> I am greatly interested in symbolic reading of the scriptures and in the Hebrew etymology of words, which reveals a very different sense from what one would initially imagine.
>
> From Genesis 2:3 I have drawn the idea that I should accept the limitations of my condition and the tenderness of God despite my disobedience. I should try to accept this life that I have received, to adapt myself to it, and to hold to my condition as a dependant creature.

You cannot get round the problem of evil: that is still a stumbling-block for me. Is it the price of our freedom? Deep down I often feel a sense of revolt... We could go on talking about it for these two years!

This ETW course is also the subject of a local radio station broadcast. There we present a few echoes of our theological work to a wider public week by week.

We could not finish this article without saying once again that the ETW is a real adventure both for the theological team and for the participants in each course, for day by day we are able to confirm that the Word requires to be reprocessed. The discoveries and definitions of yesterday cannot be repeated today for we are living and changing and our questions change with us. Such is the adventure of interpretation. As one member of ETW put it, it can take place only in "an atmosphere of friendship and readiness to listen to each other". She went on:

> For me the real work begins at the end of the meeting and goes on throughout the week. The ETW is important because it covers two years. That means organizing my time and in the long term this helps me to give the direction to my life that I want to find. At first I thought theology was dry but if I want God to communicate with me I must understand his thought, as old wine in new bottles. The ETW is important because it is not in "ritual" form. There's plenty of room left in it for discussion.

To conclude, we shall quote from another participant:

> In the ETW I feel at ease both on those days when I believe and on those when I doubt and no longer understand anything. You don't get the feeling that anyone is laying down the law. Other people's questions and difficulties, and sometimes their seeming certainty too, let me come to (new) conclusions. Understanding and community are helpful as a result of the "snippets of symbolism" contributed. They fill out the picture. This group wakes you up. In it you learn to listen to what other people have to say and nobody's opinion has pride of place. Recently I read a quotation which seems appropriate for such a forum: "'Give ear... let the earth hear the words of the Lord... as the showers upon the herb' says God" (cf. Deut. 32:1f.)[8]

NOTES

[1] The Atelier oecuménique de théologie (Ecumenical Theological Workshop) came into existence at Geneva in 1973 as a result of the desire of some friends, priests and pastors, who were anxious to "make theology available to the people of God". The course runs for two years in weekly two-hourly periods of training of work in groups, and is catered for by

a team of ten Roman Catholic and Protestant theologians, each backed by a lay animator. Each course has around one hundred members spread over two meetings (afternoon and evening).

2 Grosset, 1986.

3 The sense of the French has been retained but does not match the original Hebrew. It is the "offspring" (masculine in Hebrew) which will bruise and be bruised. Cf. Jerusalem Bible. Cf. also Good News Bible, New English Bible and RSV. (translator's note)

4 Inclusive language is used in the translation only where both sexes are unquestionably intended in the text, which begins with the *male*. (translator's note)

5 In the original the spelling is *ishah* but this does not take account of the pointing for a doubled consonant. (translator's note)

6 אִשָּׁה (ishah) is a misspelling of אִשָּׁה (ishshah) and יָה (yah) — where y = i - is a short form of יהוה (YHWH = "Yahweh"). The correspondence and contrast suggested therefore do not strictly match the data from which they are drawn in this quasi-Rabbinic type of exegesis. (translator's note)

7 Lit. "a helper as over against…" (*ezer kenegdu*). (translator's note)

8 The original quotation in the French has not been traced but could be paraphrased: "Make yourself able to understand my Word and I shall send it down like showers". (translator's note)

People Training Ministers

BRIAN HAYMES and PETER AMOS

This story has three main characters. The first is Peter. He is married to Jean and they have four daughters. In the late 1970s Peter was a school teacher but beginning to experience a call to prepare for ordination. Because he was married with a family this was full of practical difficulties but he persisted with his sense of calling and eventually found a college able to respond to his application.

The second character in the story is a local church, Mount Zion Baptist Church, Edgeside, in the Rossendale Valley, Lancashire, England. The Rossendale Valley had at one time been a great centre of Baptist church life with many lively local congregations, but ever since the first world war the churches and the economic and social life of the valley have been in decline. Mount Zion had been without ministerial leadership for some years. They had pulled down their old large building and were in the process of building a much more useful and imaginative set of premises created to serve the immediate community in which the church was set.

The third character in the story is the Northern Baptist College in Manchester, England. The college, under the principalship of Michael Taylor, had long realized both the possibilities and limitations of traditional residential training of ministers. An alternative pattern of training was devised that involved the student from the start of his or her course becoming the minister in a local congregation.[1] Clearly such students would already have had considerable church experience because they were going to be in positions of responsibility with others in the local church. Such a pattern of training would involve the students working in the church while, each week, coming to college to reflect on their practice of ministry and to undertake those necessary core curriculum courses which would be part of any person's training for ministry.

Among the advantages of such a pattern of training there are two worth highlighting in this particular case. One is that training relates practice and learning in a most creative way. The student experiences ministerial leadership in and with a local congregation. That experience becomes part of the basis of theological reflection on the practice of ministry in the college and the church.

The second advantage was in the fact that members of the local church could themselves directly contribute to the formation of a minister in training. Much ministerial formation by theological colleges does not draw upon this major resource. So Peter, Mount Zion Baptist Church and the Northern Baptist College became partners in ministerial formation.

The scheme worked in this way. If you imagine each day having three units, morning, afternoon and evening, and each week therefore possessing 21 units, the pattern of training which evolved allowed for 8 units in any one week being spent either in college or formal study, 8 further units for the practice of ministry in the local church, the remaining 5 units being at the discretion of the student. The college was particularly conscious that several students had a family and a vocation to marriage and parenthood. The 8 units of time that the student had for college study involved coming to Manchester each week where there were the usual courses one would associate with training for ministry and also the opportunity to reflect on the experiences of ministry, such as pastoral dilemmas, questions in leadership of worship and issues that arose in the community life. The college was quick to call in others who were skilled in particular areas with insights and experience beyond those of the staff to help the student think through the practice of ministry. The 8 units of time spent with the church were at the discretion of the church and student to work out together. This was a new experience for Mount Zion because previously when they had had a minister they had let him get on with whatever he thought was appropriate. Now, since there was a limited amount of time, the church with their student minister had to think about how best he as a resource would be used. This drew the church into thinking about ministry in a way that they had never had to face before.

One particular feature came to have great importance in this pattern of training. A support group of church members was convened to work particularly with Peter at the task of ministry. This support group, composed of five members of the church, not all of them church leaders and one of them a comparatively new convert, met regularly with Peter to talk over his own experience, his dreams, the things he would like to try out, the developments he would hope the church would make. At least twice a year members of the college staff came and talked with the group about Peter's development, about progress being made in the church, about the pattern of training itself, where it was working and where it wasn't. Once a year all of the churches sharing this pattern of training with the college came to the college for a day together. On these occasions a number of themes in the practice of ministry would be taken up, such as worship, pastoral care and education. The issues were identified and check lists prepared for one another on what, overall, we were trying to achieve in ministerial formation. These church group days were particularly helpful to all concerned, not least to the college. It made the staff reappraise something of their own assumptions about training. It was not that they were letting the church dictate to the college what the members thought ministers ought to be like but it was a mutual exercise in listening and dialogue to the enrichment of all.

Two particular features of Peter's experience in training and ministry have their own significance in this story.

Within a few months of his being at Mount Zion, Peter was faced with a pastoral issue of some magnitude. A young man, we shall call him Alec, a son of church members, was discovered to be a heroin addict. Peter tried to locate what help might be available for Alec and his family but there seemed to be very little, not least from the statutory services.

Peter raised this issue in a general way at the weekly report session at the college, respecting the confidentiality of those concerned. The staff and students in his group talked about the social, moral and theological issues which had arisen for Peter and some suggestions were made out of the shared experience of the group. It proved to be a long story Peter told over many weeks, of Alec attending a detoxification unit and then a community in the south of England with which some of the college members had contact. This was not altogether successful since Alec did not like where he was and became unsettled.

Peter kept close to the parents, trying to support them in days when they were optimistic and at those other moments when they were in despair. Members of the church were aware that there was grief here, without knowing the details. They also gave support and care to the parents. It was obvious to Peter that this basic pastoral response meant a lot.

Eventually Alec was to come home, when Peter and others spent a good deal of time with him. He became a helper in the youth club and, cutting the story short, Alec came to be independent of the drug.

In the meantime, Peter and others had come to realize that there was a significant "drug problem" in the valley. He came across other parents in a Baptist church with a child in similar trouble. He began to talk with them about the causes of all this and what possible supportive help might be made available. He talked about this experience with the staff and students and it became a regular "test case" for theological reflection about mission and ministry at the college. Eventually, with the knowledge and support of the parents, Peter raised the issue in the deacons and church members meetings at Mount Zion. Again cutting much discussion short, the church encouraged the setting up of a group which came to be called Parents in Pain. The church members gave financial support for a telephone care line as well as much encouragement and prayer. Three telephone lines were established eventually.

Parents in Pain meets monthly, averaging ten people at each session. Participants have come and gone as they have themselves determined. The group membership soon became ecumenical and later included those who had no church connection but certainly had the need of such a group. In a natural way spiritual resources were shared. Very few of those who used the telephone lines came to the group meetings.

The people of Mount Zion have come to see that this is a special form of ministry for some of them to engage in and for all of them to support. This is part of their calling in God's mission. They responded to their minister's growing awareness and gave him space to explore appropriate responses. From the first Peter has seen this as a ministry of the whole church. Several members have played significant parts. They have built up a dossier, edited fact sheets and gathered information about the various agencies where addicts can receive help. At the same time, they have developed relationships with the local statutory agencies who have themselves become more responsive to the problem. The group has a representative on the local advisory committee of the health authority. The church has also taken up the moral, social, economic and medical issues with local members of parliament and government ministers.

In different ways, for Peter, the church and the college, this was an important experience. As Peter talked this through with students and staff it became what it was, a real test for creative discipleship and healing. For the church members, it was a significant time of growth in understanding and practice of pastoral care as an expression of God's mission. For Peter, it was a genuine expression of "bearing one another's burdens and so fulfilling the law of Christ". This experience of collaborative contextual theological training was rich for all concerned.

The second feature of Peter's training relates to a different kind of need which emerged in the valley.

As it happend, soon after Peter became student minister at Mount Zion a number of other ministers moved out of the valley to new pastorates. In his studies Peter had come to appreciate the biblical emphasis on the corporateness of ministry, the variety of gifts of the one Spirit for building up the body of Christ (Eph. 4). He also knew that some models of ministry so centred on the minister that the gifts given to other church members were smothered under clerical dominance.

There were eleven congregations in the valley and three ministers. Peter saw that one way to respond to this situation was to help those already in the churches to discover and develop their gifts in ministry. It was no answer to stand still wringing your hands. So Peter brought this theme to the joint deacons meetings which had been started some years before. A first priority was to maintain the worship offered by the congregations in ways which were honouring to God.

Peter took the initiative with others in setting up a training course for those encouraged by their local congregations to take some responsibility for leading worship. An initial six weeks of evening meetings laid the foundations. Tutors from the college were among those who came to teach and help. Some basic theology was explored about the nature and practice of worship.

After this "foundation course" the group went on meeting monthly devising its own programme out of its own need and experience. Issues that had arisen in the work they were doing set the agenda. In this, Peter was employing locally a style of formation and learning he was undergoing in the college. About thirty people shared the course, some of whom had never had this kind of responsibility in the church before.

The following year pastoral care was the topic. Again the local churches were agents in setting up the course and encouraging, from their own memberships, those who would share it. This time about sixty participated. The earlier pattern was followed. There were six consecutive weeks of foundational themes and then the monthly self-programming. The eleven churches were encouraged to develop their own patterns of pastoral care. Once again, college staff were among those who helped the course members begin to develop listening and other skills in pastoral ministry. Fundamentally it was an exercise in shared pastoral theology and practice.

The valley churches have grown stronger through these years. Many have found a new sense of being the church, not so dependent on the minister and more aware of their own shared calling. Some have become partners with the college, like Mount Zion, in this pattern of ministerial training. Others have developed different patterns of ministry. There is a new awareness of a common calling as ecumenical links have grown.

This was not the first involvement of the college in the churches of the valley. A few years before Peter's training began the staff of the college had been invited to undertake a survey of the churches and, with local leaders, to make proposals for future developments. Four recommendations were made:

1) that there should be more training for local leaders;
2) that local ministers should be encouraged to work in all the churches;
3) that a training centre in the valley should be set up;
4) that the local churches should form a council in order to plan and work together more constructively.

The report was received but, for whatever reasons, nothing much was done except the formation of the joint deacons meeting. What has come later is a response similar to that recommended. Mount Zion has released Peter for some of his time to work with other congregations to help them discover their own God-given resources.

This story is an ongoing one. Peter is still the minister at Mount Zion Baptist Church, still developing a model of ministry which engages the membership of the church in the task of thinking through the church's calling, working at the faith by which they live. The style of ministry in leadership and decision-making is collaborative as befits Christian discipleship. A way of training is reflected in a pattern of ministry.

NOTE

[1] For a description of this pattern of training see articles by Michael Taylor in *Ministerial Formation*, July 1978 and July 1983.

They Threw me
Out of the Church

JAMES M'NAMIE and RODNEY HODGINS

James M'Namie is married with six children. His wife, Christine, is a staff nurse at Nkhata Bay District Hospital in the Northern region of Malawi. James is a self-supporting evangelist at Mpamba, a hamlet on the Mzuzu-Nkhata Bay road. This is his story, written with the assistance of Rodney Hodgins.

I was born into a Christian home. My father was a church elder in the Church of Central Africa Presbyterian (CCAP). When the missionaries decided to open mission stations in North East Rhodesia, my father was one of those who offered to go. He was one of the group which included Kenneth Kaunda's father, David. In those pioneer days mission work had a high casualty rate. My mother was one of those who succumbed to illness, leaving my father to bring up three children. I was the only son among the three.

My father sent me home to Bandawe to begin my primary education. At that time Bandawe was still a major station of the Livingstonia mission, a mission deservedly famous for its educational institutions. I boarded at the Bandawe school from 1934 to 1936, then taught for 4 years at a Church of Scotland school at Mchioroma.

When an opportunity came to train as a medical assistant in the colonial service, I applied for it. After completing my training at the old capital city of Zomba, I left Malawi for South Africa where I worked for five years. At that time salaries were very low in Malawi and many Malawians went outside for work. Labour was our biggest export in those years.

In South Africa, there were many opportunities to advance oneself. It was while there that I became interested in what I might describe as "self-improvement". I attended the Cape Technical College and studied by correspondence for my junior certificate. However, at that time I received news that my step-mother was dead and I returned home.

After a couple of years, I decided to go to Zambia and look for a post as a medical assistant. I remained in Zambia, working as a medical assistant, until 1959. The closing years of the decade were very exciting times for Africans. A federation had been imposed on the territories of Northern Rhodesia (Zambia) and Nyasaland (Malawi) in 1953. The federation linked these two territories with Southern Rhodesia. Historically, the two northern territories, Northern Rhodesia and Nyasaland, had always been treated differently from Southern Rhodesia. Although all three territories were nominally under British rule, Southern Rhodesia was self-governing and dominated by its large white population. Zambia and Nyasaland had been governed through the Colonial Office in London and the interests of Africans were regarded as paramount. When the federation was imposed, it was done without support from Africans and deliberately to increase the power of white settlers in the territories where they were few in number.

In 1958, Dr Hastings Banda returned to Malawi after an absence of some forty years. He was the most articulate Malawian of his time and had for many years financially supported the Nyasaland African Congress from abroad. However, the dramatic failure of the African opposition to the Federation convinced Dr Banda that he should return home and organize opposition himself. Within a year of his return the political situation had developed (or deteriorated, depending on your point of view) to such an extent that the federal government decided to arrest all the political leaders in Malawi, including Dr Banda.

I mention all this because it may be hard for people today to appreciate the excitement which gripped Africans at that time. This was something we experienced as community — a moment in history which I don't think will be repeated. I was in Northern Rhodesia when news of the arrests reached me. My own district, Nkhata Bay, was one of those most affected by the government action. I resigned my job and returned home to see what I could do to help in the crisis.

When I reached home, I found the Nyasaland African Congress had been banned and all political activity was at a standstill. Within weeks, however, the Malawi Congress Party was born and political action resumed. I was made district organizing secretary and spent many hours helping to rebuild the party. After some months the crisis passed. Dr Banda was released from prison and a negotiated independence rapidly followed.

Shortly before independence in 1964, I was offered a chance to train as a magistrate in the new Malawian Civil Service. For ten years I served as a magistrate in various parts of the country. Sadly, in the 1970s there were some upheavals in the country. I was one of those who spent some time in prison. They were difficult years and we thank God those things are behind us now. When I was released I worked for three years as a solicitor's clerk in Lilongwe, now the capital city, and later in Mzuzu, which is near my own home.

In telling this story so far, I have mentioned nothing of my own Christian faith. I have said little because there was little to say. Although I was a member of the CCAP like my father, I had no personal commitment to Jesus Christ. During all these years, and while I was a magistrate, Christianity was a nominal thing. Shortly before my job as a magistrate ended, a friend of mine approached me with a business proposition. He suggested that I turn a house which I owned into a bar. I agreed and a business soon developed.

While in prison one night, I had a dream. Many Africans believe in dreams and God often speaks through this channel today just as in biblical times. In my dream I saw a woman enter a church. She was very drunk and tried to interrupt the service with shouting. The preacher, a minister I knew from home, asked: "Who is this woman?" Someone answered: "She is the wife of M'Namie". The minister became very angry and called me out of the pew. He shouted at me: "Why is this so?" all the time slapping me on the face. I broke down and confessed: "It's my fault."

I awoke from my dream at that moment and went on my knees. I asked forgiveness for the sins I had committed and vowed that if I were released from prison I would serve the Lord for the rest of my life. That same month, I was released.

One of the first things I did on leaving prison was to go to Bandawe to the minister I had seen in my dream and tell him all that had happened. He helped me in those spiritual things about which I knew so little and a great hunger to know the Word of God grew in me. Fortunately, the CCAP and the Anglican church had begun a theological education by extension (TEE) programme the previous year. I was among the first students in the Northern Region. A short time later I was appointed a presbytery evangelist by the CCAP. I received no formal training other than through the TEE programme, and none was necessary.

As a presbytery evangelist, my duties involved visiting the sick, taking funerals, following up people who had made a commitment to Christ and supervising a church congregation. I was in charge of a congregation in a very poor part of the country. The monthly givings had fallen to less than $20. By encouraging the people and helping them organize stewardship campaigns, the givings rose to over $50 a month. This was sufficient for them to support their own minister.

Around this time, several para-church groups began working in Malawi. There had always been organizations closely associated with the mainstream churches, such as the Bible Society and Scripture Union, but in the 1970s new groups began to operate. Some of these are well known internationally, such as Every Home Crusade and New Life for All, but they were new to Malawi and the churches tended to be somewhat suspicious of them. Many church members were attracted to these groups because they had a spiritual vitality that was often lacking in the denominational services. It's hard even now to see why there was such opposition to these groups; they were what I might call very traditional evangelical. The emphasis was on Bible study and outreach, hardly radical departures from mainstream Christianity!

I used to attend these meetings, and served for a time on the committee of Every Home Crusade. We used to organize after church meetings and visit people in their houses for Bible study and prayer. The "official" church didn't like these groups. It was said that they were trying to form a church within a church. In my own Presbyterian church, meetings of session took place where the elders involved in these groups were questioned about their activities. Eventually the meetings were stopped and church members forbidden to be involved in such things.

The sad thing was that many young men within the church were getting involved in beer-drinking and womanizing. There was no other entertainment available to them. After church services there was no activity provided for them. Up till now, this continues to be the case. The desire to hear and learn the Word of God was evident, but no provision was made for it. Some of us suggested to the minister that he should start his own Bible study group and we would support him in running it, but he wasn't interested. By the time I became a full-time presbytery evangelist, many of the young men who had been active in these para-church groups had given up their involvement, fearing discipline or suspension by their churches.

It wasn't only para-church groups that provoked the opposition of professional churchmen. In the area where I come from we managed to sustain a schism which no longer has point or purpose. The schism took place in the old Presbyterian mission church when the first ordained African minister broke away from the mission church to form his own church, known as the Blackman's Church of Central Africa Presbyterian (BCCAP). As can be guessed from the title, the schism was rooted in the frustrations many Africans felt over the domineering attitude of some European missionaries.

Unfortunately, even though the mission church was handed over even before independence to African control, it has proved impossible to heal the rift. The CCAP and the BCCAP have no formal dealings with each other. Of course, this being Africa, on the social level people have to live in community and so everyone gets on very happily in the village, but go their separate ways to church. The quarrel does become quite bitter at times, especially at funerals which are always a good excuse to engage in polemics against the opposite party.

It must be said that not all CCAP ministers are equally opposed to their brothers in the BCCAP. When TEE in Malawi (TEEM) started in the Nkhata Bay area, a minister of the CCAP was asked to be the tutor/facilitator. He agreed to do that, and because TEEM is an ecumenical body he welcomed members of the BCCAP to his tutorials. Everything went on like that for some years, until someone took exception to a remark made by a minister of the BCCAP to the effect that the two churches were the same because both were using the same training programme. A row developed and it was decided that no CCAP minister should tutor BCCAP students. There were threats of disciplining ministers who disobeyed.

The TEEM staff arranged separate tutorials for the BCCAP students and that continued to be the case for a time. Eventually TEEM was told not to help these people any more and because TEEM is owned by the CCAP, they had to obey. It is even harder to understand this attitude when you realize that BCCAP members are living and working with these same CCAP ministers every day of the week. They enter each other's houses and often come from the same extended families. It's not right to blame the CCAP for this, I think the attitude is there in all churches. If you look for it, you will nearly always find it.

In many ways the relationship of the TEE programme to the mainstream churches has been a strange one. The churches themselves began this programme and they remain the owners of it. The staff members are all seconded from the mainstream churches themselves. Despite this, there have always been suspicions about TEE in the congregations.

For example, one of the requirements a TEE student must fulfill is to engage in some practical work in his own parish. In our churches in Malawi, most of the preaching is done by church elders and lay people. It cannot be otherwise as ministers are few in number. When I tried to arrange for TEE students to preach at their churches, I found that there was much opposition. Sometimes this opposition came from ministers and at other times from church elders. Of course, always there were excuses. A student might be refused permission to preach because the preaching rota was already drawn up and such like. In many of our churches elders are chosen because of the positions they hold in the community. Many of these men are ill-equipped to minister the Word of God and have little interest in getting equipped for ministry. To these men, TEE is a threat rather than an opportunity.

Similar problems arise when TEE tutor/facilitators are appointed. In my own case, when I had finished my studies I was asked to lead a group near my own home. The parish minister had refused to help this group as he complained he had no time. We used to meet twice every month for about three hours on a Saturday morning. When the parish minister realized that the group was functioning on a regular basis he was annoyed. He didn't like to see his church members being taught by the church evangelist. When the time came for the students to write their examination, the minister complained to the church session. He said that no one had asked his permission for these exams to take place. He later wrote to the presbytery and complained that I was neglecting my duties as an evangelist by spending so much time on the TEE work. Nothing much came of the complaints, but it made things very difficult for everybody. I don't think there was any substance to what he was saying. It was a straightforward case of the professional theologian protecting his privilege of speaking for God to the people.

For some years, I had harboured an ambition to become ordained myself and serve the church as a "professional" minister. In 1983, it seemed my chance had come. The synod of Livingstonia recognized that there was an acute shortage of ministers in the parishes and decided to run a two-year emergency course which would set aside the regulations on academic qualifications and age. I applied to be one of the students on this emergency course.

After some weeks, I was called to an interview and an examination. I was successful in the examination and the interview seemed to go quite well. I had every hope of being selected. However, each presbytery had to sponsor the name of the candidates from within its area. In the case of my own presbytery, this meant that some of those ministers who were unhappy about my involvement with TEE and other para-church groups had an opportunity to block my entry to the emergency course.

Although I was very disappointed at the time, I realize now that it should have been no surprise to me when I heard I had been refused. I was too old!

Despite the setback to my plans of becoming an ordained minister, I continued with my work as a presbytery evangelist. I resolved to be as effective a lay minister as I might ever have been an ordained minister. There was no shortage of opportunities as a great hunger exists in Malawi for Christian things. When I heard of a major crusade which was being organized in our region, I decided to attend the preparatory meetings. Gradually, I became involved in the organization of the crusade and was asked to be coordinator for our district. This work involved following up people who made commitments to Christ and helping them to join local churches.

The CCAP has always been wary of working with outside evangelists. The church runs its own evangelism campaigns and these have been very successful over the years. When the church discussed the Christ for All Nations Crusade to be led by Reinhard Bonnke, they decided not to get involved as a denomination. However, in some congregations ministers criticized the idea of a crusade and threatened to discipline church members who attended. It was said, a familiar complaint this, that Bonnke was trying to start "a church within a church". In my own congregation some people talked of me as a "Bonnke man".

The crusade was quite successful, attracting large numbers of people. When it was over, the crusade team went elsewhere and those of us who had been involved in the preparations set about the task of following up the people who had made commitments. A good number of these were our own CCAP people, but this seemed to increase the hostility of some towards the evangelist and his crusade team.

A presbytery meeting decided to forbid CCAP members from active participation in organizing crusades or the activities of "outside" groups. I tried to say that men and women like myself supported such groups because we were helped by the spiritual vitality we found there.

It was clear that my own position in the CCAP was becoming increasingly difficult. I was accused of teaching that infant baptism was wrong. I answered by pointing to the example of my own children, all of whom had been baptized as infants and never rebaptized. It was said that I was against baptism by sprinkling and that I had told this to a youth group at a rally. I tried to explain that I was asked about baptism by immersion and that I had replied that the only examples given in scripture were of baptism by immersion. However, there was a feeling that I was no longer interested in being a CCAP evangelist, and I was told that the presbytery no longer needed my services.

When I returned home, I sat down and tried to think out my own position. I knew that I would continue my involvements with para-church groups and that eventually I would be suspended from church membership for it. I felt it would be a disappointment to many if they heard that I had been suspended from the CCAP. They would think it was for some moral failure and be discouraged in their own lives. Better that I should resign from the CCAP and go my own way than be suspended for doing something I feel to be right. That is how I came to leave my church.

So now, what do I feel about my TEE studies which in some way have led me out of the church I had worshipped with from childhood? What I feel is that TEE has played a major role in directing my spiritual life. In terms of knowledge, TEE has been so successful in equipping me for ministry that even ordained ministers have recognized the worth of what has been done.

What makes me sad is that there is now a repetitive cycle to church life. People are baptized and later confirmed as church members and it ends there. We have members who practise the old things they used to practise before they entered the Christian church, and naturally such people don't like talk of being born again or of people being filled with the Holy Spirit. TEE encourages people to get together and ask themselves "what does it mean to follow Christ?"

TEE does help Christians understand the Word of God and look beyond the minister to the Christ and, without realizing it, many professional ministers dislike TEE because of that. They would prefer to remain the one who tells people what they should do. TEE helped me, and others like me, to recognize what is right and what is wrong in the practice of ministry.

How they Read the Bible in Isolotto

IAN FRASER *Rules*

Some time ago I was asked to write an article on how basic Christian communities had begun in Latin America and then spread to the rest of the world. I wrote back saying I was prepared to write an article to show that the development was different. What happened was something like spontaneous combustion of the Spirit. In many parts of the world one found the coming into being of communities which had different styles and emphases, because they took seriously the different contexts in which they were set — then their discovery of one another and the making of community with one another — in which process they found that, for all their differences, they had deep marks of kinship and common features which were a sign that the one Spirit had brought them into being.

The Bible is given a place of fundamental importance in all basic Christian communities. There is a great freshness of interpretation when people escape from class and clergy-caste interpretation traps which had previously monopolized. The new place of the poor is not just a slogan — the poor have a vantage point for interpreting scripture which gives fresh access to the biblical message. This is not because the poor are uncontaminated by sin. It is because they adopt the same ground for their perceptions as the one who had nowhere to lay his head, whose companions were outcasts, who suffered oppression and death.

All over the world, the church is being built up by a sharing of insights and perceptions provided by those who search to live the faith in different cultural and social contexts. The sharing is important. In Oporto, a young girl shared with my wife and myself the imaginative interpretation of the community to which she belonged of Jesus' word that he came to bring not peace but a sword: "We believe Jesus was saying to his own people and is saying to us that the poor are not meant to sit down passively under oppression but to get up on their hind legs and counter the oppression."

This insight from Portugal chimes in with the Latin American experience. Wherever the church had taught over centuries that the poor should accept suffering and oppression with resignation, saying of themselves "we are just the poor and humble of the earth", they needed to be liberated into the realization that they were made in the image of God, had a place in God's world and a share in shaping their own destiny, and so should not sit down fatalistically but get up and fight. Experience and biblical interpretation could enrich each other across the Atlantic. Again in Oporto, Manuela put succinctly a perception of her community of the role of the Virgin Mary in some such way as this: "As we studied the Bible, we came to be aware that Mary's virginity lay not in a physical intactness but in her being asked to have a child who would not be her own." Again in Latin America, but also in many other parts of the world, Mary as she is in the scriptures is being recovered from the clutches of the official church which, over so many years, presented her as a model of uncomplaining patience and resignation. If women are to be freed from stereotyping in the church of the future, then Mary has to be freed from stereotype interpretations of her role.

The Bible makes fresh impact through processes which have a clear thread of development. The start will often be a kind of discomfort in the Spirit regarding the way in which realities encountered in the world and the words of scripture contradict one another. Working this through can lead to a point where a key question has to be addressed to the Bible and some thorough work done on biblical sources. Thereafter there has to be an exposition-into-life to express and complete the exposition-into-words. This simple line of development can be used to illustrate the way in which basic Christian communities all over the world are facing the problem of power structures in the church and have made discoveries which can be usefully shared across the board with one another and with the wider church.

Wherever basic Christian communities came into being, you would find a discomfort in the Spirit regarding the role of hierarchical, bureaucratic, clergy in-between structures. There is no sign of these in scripture. Those who have particular pastoral and leadership responsibilities are part of the body, dependent on other functioning organs and contributing to their life. There is no "clergy-neck" between the Head and the Body, connecting each to the other and interpreting each to the other. So it is with other pictures in scripture. The church is like a building made up of lively stones, each contributing to its strength. The church is like a household or family in which the members can be as different as chalk and cheese, yet use that difference to enrich the unity. The church is like a vine with branches — and the branches are the members (at times it would look as if official representatives were the branches and the members only twigs or offshoots). The church is like a bride prepared for her husband. The church is God's field. And so on. In order to get a special position for leaders, especially ordained leaders, especially bishops and archbishops, the picture of a shepherd and the flock has been fastened on in much of history. But it is Christ who is the definitive Shepherd. The sign of that shepherding is giving up life, not administering or pastoring. At best, those who have particular responsibilities are "under-shepherds", "feeders of the flock". There is simply no warrant in scripture for the existence of a clergy-caste.

As the Trinity is in the shape of a circle (note the 15th-century Russian icon of Rublev) so the church has been designed to take the form of a circle. At the foot-washing, Jesus pointed out that his lordship was expressed in forms of humble service. How then have pyramids of power developed in the church and what are we to do with them? That is a question being faced by basic Christian communities in almost every part of the world (because, when the form of a church is not overtly hierarchical or bureaucratic, there is so often a less visible power structure which is not very recognizable as a service structure).

The concrete question, how power is to operate in the church, faced basic communities all over the world in different ways. Sometimes hierarchies and bureaucracies appreciated the development "from below", made space for it and encouraged it. Sometimes hierarchies and bureaucracies did their best to ignore, isolate or eliminate such communities. In either case, it seemed that one was not free simply to "be church" or "live church" — phrases which in the communities replaced the "going to church" way of expressing allegiance and discipleship: you got the hierarchy on your side or you found it confronting you or you ducked under its arms and got on with the job. Why was this bloc there?

The Isolotto community, an artisan community on the outskirts of Florence, undertook a thorough bit of study and research which threw light on the situation. This work was made available in extensive form, but was also summarized as follows:

Isolotto reads the Bible
Study of the Exodus had shown:
1. The foundation of the Decalogue is God who liberates, so the Law has its origin in the same Spirit as called out a rebellion of slaves.

2. This God is also present in the people and acts through them.
3. The Decalogue is, like the Exodus, a stage towards total liberation — if not treated thus, it can be an instrument of slavery.

After working through the book of Exodus the community followed the historical itinerary of the Jewish people in the conquest and settling of Palestine: the books of Joshua and Judges.

On this second stage, the community observed: "We became aware of the danger of analyzing the events of the Bible through the moral, social and ideological categories of our culture, we recognized the temptation-danger to use only a part of the Bible in order to justify our vision of things, even if that vision were progressive and tending towards a society without classes."

The books were divided up and a part allocated to everyone who participated. When the group came to the passage, the person responsible had to present it, comment on it and highlight awkward or challenging parts of it. This method became possible only after two years of studying and struggling with biblical texts. When the community came to Leviticus, Numbers and Deuteronomy, they worked with certain chosen headings for the sake of coherence, since the text was so vast and fragmented.

One point of concentration was the priest who did the Pentateuch

Once the Hebrew people were clear of Egypt, they found it necessary to organize themselves. In Moses' absence they made a declaration for the social order based on power and wealth (the Golden Calf). Moses brought them to their senses, helping them to see God's requirements for society.

In Exodus the priesthood has a limited place. There is no institutionalizing of a system of offerings — once the people have given what is necessary for the tabernacle and ark and their fittings, the people are asked to stop bringing offerings. The Levites had a specific function only in suppressing the adoration of the Golden Calf and administering the people's offerings when the ark was being built. The first sacrifice took place at the foot of Sinai at the conclusion of the alliance and was carried out by "some young men of the people of Israel" (Ex. 24:4-7). The priesthood was born in service of the people's needs along the path of liberation. Even in Leviticus as in Exodus, there is no reference to a sacred role carried out by the Levites, the only priesthood is that of Aaron and his family.

It was part of a slow historical process that a privileged priestly caste took over. Note Amos 5:21-25 where sacrifices and offerings are put in their place in relation to justice. The life of the people becomes controlled by rites and sacrifices to God, the animals being in perfect condition, from which the priests would also benefit. The best of everything is to go to the priests now (Num. 18:8-13). Whereas sin had been exclusively the betrayal of the pact of alliance between God and the people in Exodus, in Leviticus it gets associated with ritual uncleanness and purifying. Jeremiah (7:21-23) says: "But in the day that I brought them out of the land of Egypt, I did not speak to your fathers or command them concerning burnt offerings and sacrifices. But this command I gave them: 'Obey my voice, and I will be your God, and you shall be my people; and walk in all the way I command you that it may be well with you.'"

Finally, the priests have themselves to be unblemished, not handicapped or mutilated or deformed.

In Numbers and Deuteronomy God is seen as consecrating an entire tribe, that of Levi, to care for the tabernacle and the sacred things. They could not be priests and hence could not make offerings and sacrifices. That tribe was not allowed to possess land or real estate and hand these over to the next generation; and did not have its own region but lived in cities in the various regions. It could have been an element of union. Leviticus 8:14-19 shows the Levites were consecrated to God in place of the first-born. These, spared when the first-born of Egypt was slain, were meant to inherit the legacy of a previous generation for the support of the family, and to transmit to the next generation the alliance between God and the people for liberation and salvation.

The priestly apparatus became a power apparatus. Jesus chased out the profaners from the temple and spoke of the master of the vineyard in a way which revealed to the priests and Pharisees that he was speaking about them. He was against the infidelity of the priesthood in respect of its original and genuine spirit. He warned that such a priesthood would be destroyed.

* * *

What can be seen from the Isolotto research is that an enabling structure can become an in-between, dominating power structure and in the process can make fish and flesh of those who are members of the people of God, disinheriting notably women, the handicapped and the poor. The study presents a pattern of integrated living and different forms of service — which changes under the pressure of a felt need for religious status, security and power. Does this give a clue to the rise of in-between power structures in the church which change it from the shape of a circle to the shape of a pyramid? If this is so, what is to be done? Is the pyramid to be opposed and brought crashing down, or circumvented and bypassed, or changed wherever it is not at the service of the people of God and thence of the world?

As the liturgy of worship must lead to the liturgy of life so exposition of the Bible and Word must lead to exposition in practice. Sometimes as the result of intuition, sometimes spurred by clear indicators from scripture, sometimes as a result of thorough research such as Isolotto's, the base Christian communities have restored the shape of a circle.

a) The French base Christian communities were particularly sensitive to the possibility that their form of life might allow a new structure of power to be erected. To begin with, when they sprouted all over the place, they had little contact with one another in case the very act of coordinating produced a new power-centre (Georges Casalis said: "We are all congregationalists!") The publication "Nouvelles de communautés" was located in Paris, then shifted to Toulouse, then to Lyon, then back to the Paris area because of the worry that a new power-base might be created at one place. Not until the third National Assembly of base Christian communities did representatives of communities from all over France become convinced that institutionalizing is necessary in order that there might be sharing and building up of the communities in the faith they lived, through mutual support and criticism; and this institutionalizing need not be the top-heavy kind which produces dominating blocs of power but can be a light institutionalizing in a servant form. So it was agreed that there should be a continuing national coordinating resource for France. Such a resource is sometimes called a "technical secretariat" to make it clear that it is simply a functional service which is offered, with no special status attached. So the attempt is being made in the development of base Christian communities in France to build in a form of coordination which will be carefully invigilated to prevent it sliding from being a serving, enabling structure to becoming an in-between, dominating power structure.

b) In Italy exposition-in-practice is expressed not only in a technical secretariat but also in a growth of worker-priests and worker-pastors. Ordained clergy who might have formed an in-between body are relocated and relocate themselves so that they are in the mainstream of life and share the experience, suffering, joys of other members of the people of God, especially poorer ones. They do work with little status and low pay, or they are unemployed alongside the unemployed. Those whom I have questioned said they would never go back to the unreal location they were previously given by the official church which kept them out of the mainstream of life. In the mainstream, in the community to which they belong, they have no special voice, no last word. Yet there they can contribute to the community's understanding of the faith lived in both their scholarship and the gifts of their training. It is when the ordained lose their separateness and their separate visibility and set their skills alongside the skills for working and suffering with the rest of the community that they look like organs in the body again instead of some separated caste. This amounts to a deliberate redesigning of priesthood in the way in which Isolotto has shown it originated in the Old Testament to replace the priesthood which Jesus found in his day — which, in him, was given its death-blow in favour of the priesthood of the whole people of God.

c) In the Ipil diocese in Mindanao in the Philippines, hierarchy has been redesigned. Think of a pyramid changed into a spiral and then pressed down so that it becomes a spring — and you have some understanding of the change which has been made. It would seem that one had to choose between the church in the form of a circle or with a hierarchy — but here is a hierarchy designed in the form of a circle! This is how it functions.

In the diocese there are around 1,200 basic Christian communities, each drawing on six or eight households. These examine alertly the developing situation — often marked by military pressure — in the immediate surroundings where their homes are; and they search the scriptures using a study-resource which they and the scholars have worked out together. Once a week they gather their insights and prayers into a "capilya" service, conducted by a lay person who presides over a reserved sacrament.

Once a month the leaders appointed by local communities meet in "zonas" for about two days to keep one another up to scratch about the leadership they are offering (are they being secretly manipulated?) and to get built up more adequately in an understanding of the Bible. So those who hold that kind of responsibility are being equipped to fulfill it.

Six times a year a representative from each "zona" and the presidents of chapel worship take part in a parish meeting which allow them to assess what is happening over a wider area. A wider area is the district which gathers into it the thinking and concerns of four parishes. It meets quarterly.

Finally the spring tightens and centres itself on a prelature assembly which offers about 150 representatives the opportunity to look at the diocese and its whole needs and priorities, four times per year. Priests and religious are in a minority in the steering committee and the bishop does not even preside — an appointed lay person does. He may contribute from the floor and he retains an authoritative position in the community, all the more so since he acts as a servant, not as a lord.

Once the prelature assembly has taken place, the spring unwinds back to the local basic Christian communities which get their perceptions enlarged by what is happening over the diocese as a whole and are inspired by a sense of a whole body working organically under the Spirit.

The main advice which hierarchies and bureaucracies need to hear is "Let go! God will provide what is needed." At the time of the celebration of the first anniversary of the success of the revolution in Nicaragua, I lived in the "barrio Ciudad Sandino" in a small Jesuit community which lived at the level of the people. My resource person was Paco who had been my contact with communities in Paraguay when he was serving there. I asked him what it was like to have basic Christian communities developing in that area. He said:

> We were scared. We were really scared. We saw all that we had been trained and ordained for disappearing into the people and thought that nothing might be left for us. Was preaching our task? The people building one another up in an understanding of the Bible and the faith through the experiences of seeking to live it in a pressured situation each day were far better preachers than we could aspire to be. Was worship then our responsibility? The people lifting to God their struggles and sufferings and praising God with joy and hope in the midst of it all, developed worship full of reality for which we as ordained could offer no substitute. At least the Mass was in our control? We very soon became convinced that it was the action of the people together. We thought there would be nothing left for us. We seriously considered the question whether we should try to pull things back into our own court before they got lost altogether.
>
> "And what did you do?" I asked.
>
> "We just had enough grace to let it go," said Paco. "And what happened?" "In no time at all the people had given back a place to us not over them but with them so that we have rediscovered ministry together."

Theology by the Young People in Brazil

JACI MARASCHIN and KLÉCIO DOS SANTOS

Violence, censorship and political and ideological repression in Brazil reached their zenith between 1968 and 1975 when the military government would not allow any kind of opposition. At this moment, 1988, the country lives in a sort of a supposed transition from the military regime to a hopefully more democratic way of life. However, even if tortures are not so much visible as before, and censorship is much less obvious, nothing guarantees that they are over. Very recently the president of the Brazilian Republic did prohibit by decree the exhibition of the controversial film by the French director Jean-Luc Godard, "Je vous salue Marie", at the request of the Roman Catholic authorities. This was done without any regard to the cultural and artistic opinion of people. The same climate of repression is still visible in our streets when workers, students and teachers come out to fight for better wages.

In this climate of repression we, professor Maraschin and student Klécio, met on the occasion of an Anglican congress in Panama, and shared some thoughts which we want to develop in this article. Maraschin teaches theology at the Ecumenical Programme of Post-Graduate Studies on Sciences of Religion in Sao Paulo, and Klécio has just started his university course in journalism in a Catholic university in Pelotas, South Brazil. Maraschin is a priest of the Anglican church in Brazil, and Klécio a member of a very conservative parish in the same denomination. The Anglican church in Brazil is, in general, a conservative body. People in that church do not like changes.

Why does a young person remain a member of the church in such conditions? We sensed the following factors:
a) they are influenced by their families in the early years of their lives;
b) then the youth movement in the churches may catch their attention;
c) sometimes the influence of a young pastor is decisive;

d) the young people, coming together, through the youth movement, create a sort of front against the old-time parish life and the moralistic approach to reality, developping their own Christian conscience.

The youth movement at the diocesan level started in South Brazil in the last two years. It was politically oriented. If in the past the themes of youth conferences and symposia were "individual prayer", "ways of sanctification", "praise of God", and so on, more recently they have shifted to "the role of the Christian people in the struggle for agrarian reform", "the new constitution of Brazil and the Christians", "the role of the church in the liberation of the poor", etc. The young people felt they belonged to the people and took this belonging seriously. They discovered that persons are able to face such questions from the perspective of the gospel and that Christians should listen to people of other faiths and of no faiths at all in order to participate in the struggle for liberation going on in Latin America.

The young people did not want to act alone, as if they were another church. So they invited the clergy of their region (South Brazil) and asked them questions such as:

a) What kind of pastoral practice do you think we should have in our diocese?

b) What is your opinion about the participation of young Christians in *party politics?* Should Christians be militant in *party politics?*

The clergy were not at ease with such questions but were eager to listen to the young people and tried to give them some help.

From this encounter with the Episcopal clergy, the young people decided to meet pastors and theologians from other denominations and discovered a new dimension of their faith through the ecumenical movement.

We tend to think of people as workers, farmers, miners, illiterate persons, all on the fringes of society. But in Brazil there are thousands of young people trying to enter university, coming precisely from these levels of society. They try hard to interpret their own condition of poverty and oppression in which their parents, relatives and friends live, through a very close kind of relationship. One of the results of their participation in the life of the country through the class and cultural struggles is the beginning of a new kind of "theology by the people".

We are affirming that the young people starting their courses in our universities are already thinking people, interpreting the sources of people's faith. These sources are, as in every place, the Bible, Tradition and the living experience of the church. However, though they are the same everywhere they may be seen, in each particular place, from different perspectives. Brazilian young people do not want to read the Bible from the standpoint of their parents, probably good some twenty years ago but not adequate now to the situation they are facing. They want to read it from the standpoint of liberation, informed by the struggles of the people in the conflicting areas of social, economic and political action.

Theology by the people is a contextual theology. Some of these young people had had in their earlier years, while still in secondary school, experiences linked to the student movement in Brazil. Around 1984 the generation born in 1968 was facing the results of an educational act called "Diretrizes e Bases" ("Orientations and Bases") issued by the military government. The chief objectives of that law can be outlined as follows: to put the student outside the political process going on in Brazil; give priority to technology and technocracy, directing education to the formation of experts in technological skills; to avoid creativity and independence in the learning process; give more attention to mathematics and physics to the detriment of the social sciences; avoid creative thinking and eliminate debates in the class room; weakening of the public school and strengthening of the private (and elitist) school; and development of fascist ideals as the doctrine of "national security" and the persecution of people not supporting the military government.

A document written by secondary students in 1985 tried to inform society about the hopes and intentions of the younger generation. It is worth quoting:

> Our generation is being silenced. Our creativity has been killed. They want to transform our schools in plants to produce technicians mild and obedient to the system. They want us to be mere servants and slaves of capitalism. They do not want us to have access to real knowledge. Our schools are supposed to be confessional boxes of imported formulations. They want us to be like a herd.
>
> The dignity of youth is constantly denied in our schools through the hideous system of teaching which subordinates the student to the authority of professors always protecting the viewpoints of the system and always condemning the dialectical possibility of any dialogue.
>
> We are forced to see in our class rooms the mutilation of history, in which members of the armed forces are always presented as heroes of the country and in which the true movements of liberation of the people are never mentioned.[1]

Some of these young students were linked to the church but had not found in the liturgy or in the preaching of their communities any relationship of the gospel to their needs and struggles. It is probable that the adult Christians had things more important to do. They were too busy with their own problems to give attention to their younger friends. Nevertheless, the young people felt they were still Christians and should fight for their right to be Christians. Perhaps, Christians of a different kind. In the small space conquered in their churches they formed small groups and enjoyed the experience of friendship and prayer together. Some of them wanted something more. They wanted to change the situation. Indeed, they looked for the possibility of relating the struggle going on in school with the church. Would the gospel have something to say in that situation? Could Christians participate in a revolutionary struggle as real as they were experiencing it in their school life?

One of the boys started a Bible study group, and the first meeting was dedicated to the interpretation of the parable of the vineyard. Matthew 20:1-16 was for many young students a very puzzling story, as it is for some of us. But when they got together to read it again and again with attention and from their own experience, they started seeing in the parable things which were at the beginning not very important. Some of them thought of the owner of the vineyard as like any Latin American owner of land today. He would go around looking for cheap labour and would not be concerned with justice. But, suddenly they realized that the owner of the vineyard had a different attitude. If he were a modern land-owner he would pay less to the men hired later. But he did not. So, for some young people this meant that the owner was not chiefly concerned about wages, or profit, but about human beings, who had the same needs even when not working for the same period of time as others. Another group of youngsters saw in the parable a lesson on unemployment. They were puzzled with the great number of people "doing nothing". They were probably waiting in the market place for some work to do. But this was not easy to get. Even the owner of the vineyard was astonished with the social situation of his country. "Why do you spend the day like that, doing nothing?" The situation was the same as in Brazil in those days (and still is the same) where unemployment is the terrible experience of thousands of men and women young and old. For some people the parable was a judgment on self-righteousness. All labour has to have social implications. The first workers thought of their work as only something done to benefit them, individually. The owner of the vineyard thought of it as something social and decided that everybody had to have the same wages because, certainly, everybody had similar needs. Of course, this was not so explicit in the parable, but for the young students there could not be found another convincing explanation.

Students wanted to know what the relationship of the Bible was to the social situation of the country. Their biblical studies had, from now on, a deep concern for liberation.

This new vision of the Christian commitment was reflected in the liturgical life of the group. Instead of thinking about matters of personal interest, prayers, songs and meditations were now linked to social questions. They brought the altar into the midst of the people. Instead of an academic sermon, not always concerned with the problems they were facing, they developed a new kind of communication, through slides, drama, movement and music. Spirituality was a matter of the totality of their lives and not only a brief moment of silence and meditation.

Young people looked for certainty. Where to find it? They found it in their biblical studies. There is in Brazil a very active group of theologians of liberation doing a remarkable job in teaching the Bible to the people. This is an ecumenical movement, called CEBI, which means Centres for Biblical Studies. It is worth noticing that young people from rural zones are more open to this kind of study than urban young people. Why? Perhaps because the urban young people are more dependent on the traditional church than rural youth.

The young people find it very difficult to understand the church. But the church provides for them some structural elements aiming at the creation of spaces for creativity, like congresses, symposia, debates, and biblical studies. On the other hand, there is always a temptation to transform these spaces into ghettos outside of the world. It is natural for some youngsters to look for clubs, closed associations, as places of refuge and protection. There is always this danger. In that case, when some youngsters discover other movements, in society, much more open to participation and more activist, they tend to leave the church.

What about theology? Do the young people have a "theological conscience"? In general, they think that theology is an outdated discipline, and for persons especially trained for that purpose. On the other hand, many young people are aware that they also may be "theologians". They are not particularly interested in the traditional doctrines of the church. They know they exist though they are not well aware about the reason. The Nicene Creed, which is regularly recited during the eucharistic liturgy in the Anglican church, is ignored. But they are interested in the person of Jesus Christ which, perhaps is much more the Jesus of Nazareth than the mystical Christ. He is seen as a revolutionary leader.

They do not pay attention to some traditional elements related to the doctrine of the person of Jesus, like the "miraculous birth" or the stories of the "ascension" or of the resurrection. They show little interest in the doctrine of the Holy Spirit. They think that this belongs to the charismatics and the charismatics do not belong to this world. Of course, this is the situation in a very specific part of the world: south Brazil. We know that in some other regions of the world the "charismatic movement" may also have political and social implications. But not here.

What kind of leadership can be seen in the youth movement as we are describing here? This leadership arises in the communities and is related to the real needs experienced in these communities. Some of the characteristics of this leadership are:

a) young people look for a very gifted and "charismatic" leader;
b) this leader has to have the gift of sharing leadership with others;
c) the leader involves the community as a whole in the different tasks to be done;
d) it allows for self-criticism.

This kind of leadership opposes models based on authority. This is very important in the Anglican church in Brazil because there is an ancient tradition of authority based on a monarchical model, which still dominates in most of our dioceses. During the realization of the Latin American Anglican Congress, in Panama in November 1987, most of the young people present denounced the monarchical model of authority.

Taking into consideration the issues which are the concern of the young people the theological education design developed by the church should, at least, stress three points:

1. Theological education has to be contextualized. It is not sufficient to have good theologians and good professors in a particular centre. We need a programme of theological education in the very place where leadership is emerging, aware of the specific realities of the region. It is not always possible to move people from one town into a big centre in order to educate theologians.

2. If, for traditional reasons, theological education has to pay attention to the historical contents of our faith (Bible, Tradition, and ecclesial experience), it has also to be concerned with the cultural atmosphere of the locality where it is studied, where social, political and economic issues develop.

3. Theological education has to be ecumenical. There are a number of resources in the many denominations in a given region. These resources can be used for the formation of leadership in the church. Besides,

there are ecumenical organizations devoted to the formation of lay people specializing in pastoral matters.

Books and theological journals are rather expensive for most of the young people who desire to participate intelligently in the life of the world and in the life of the church. The group of youngsters in south Brazil is thinking of creating a common library. This may receive the assistance of one or two leading theologians in Brazil and may prove to be a valuable tool in our programmes of lay theological education. Many young people's groups edit their own "home-made" periodicals, which are very good as far as communication is concerned. These artisan "newsletters" reach many youngsters and show where they are in their Christian commitment.

Another way of developing their theology is through poetry and music. It is very common in Brazil to find the most diverse groups of young people sharing a common interest in music and poetry. Some of them reach a high degree of excellence and produce records which are sold in the music market.

What about the ministry? We think that not only ordained people "belong" to the ministry. The ministry is "of Christ" and he calls whosoever he wants to help him in his ministry of liberation. It is good to know that the church, officially, proclaims that the "ministry" belongs to the whole people of God. But it is not easy to understand what the church means by that. We still suffer from a ministry reduced to ordained clergy which shows signs of elitism, paternalism and authoritarianism. We still have a long way to go in order to really believe that the ministry is "of the whole people of God". This is why the question of the ministry is so important in a theology made by the young people in Brazil.

There is, in Brazil, a very strong sense of hierarchy. Our churches praise it and support it. The hierarchical tradition involves many things. It has to do with the form of the liturgy, with the music we sing, with the style of our behaviour in church and in society, etc. It is in the very atmosphere.

Brazil is a machist culture. The young generation believes in the sharing of responsibilities. It is not possible to think of ministries performed only by male persons. Thanks to God, the Anglican church in Brazil is already ordaining women to the priesthood, though until this moment we have only two women priests. This was not an easy thing to achieve. There are still many people in our church convinced that this was a mistake.

Traditionally we think that the ministry of the church is reduced to the threefold ministry of bishops, presbyters and deacons. Not all youngsters want to go to the seminary to become priests. But they think they are part of the ministry of the church and should be acknowledged as such. They don't think they have to be bishops, presbyters or deacons in order to be part of that ministry. So they feel that our practice should be more inclusive. Starting from the Bible, which they are reading and studying, the church has to recognize the enormous diversity of gifts. Those gifts appear differently in different situations. It is not possible to think that one selected type of ministry can be sufficient for the exercise of all the required gifts in a specific community.

The young people are convinced that any kind of ministry has to be a ministry of liberation. Starting from their own experience of oppression, repression and dependence, most of the youngsters expect the church to assume a role of redemption. The ministry of the church is expected to be a ministry of liberation to the captives, of liberation to the oppressed from the power of oppression, of liberation of the repressed by moralistic factors, for a life of joy and fullness, of liberation from the owners of culture, to the creation of real indigenous culture, of liberation from the depersonalizing practices of technology to the freedom found in dialogue and love.

What kind of theology will serve all this? The theology by the young people is looking for that. They may not know all the methodology of the academia, but they know it in their experience and live full of hope in the future. This is theology in the making, and we do not know what will come out of it. We know, however, that the church has to be sensitive to the young people and has to listen to them.

NOTE

[1] Document circulating in a secondary school of Pelotas, RS, Brazil, printed in a news letter produced by students.

The Negro Spiritual
as People's Theology

J. OSCAR McCLOUD

The middle-aged woman sat with her eyes closed, her head tilted back slightly, and nodding back and forth in assent to the baritone as he sang "He is king of Kings, He is Lord of Lords; Jesus Christ, The First and Last, no man works like him." This Black sister of the faith knew the reality of Revelation 17:14 in a way which required neither preacher nor theologian. The scene is repeated in many Black churches across the United States of America when Black people gather to worship, and to sing the music known as the Negro spiritual. Worship in the Black congregations continues to express a view of the life of the people which is symbolized in the Negro spiritual. The spiritual, which originated among Black slaves in the USA, is one of the few authentic forms of American music. For Black Americans, the Negro spiritual (it simply doesn't sound right to say the "Black spiritual") continues to be a relevant form of expression of the Black Christians' thoughts about God, their circumstances in this world, and their hopes for the life to come.

It is not possible here to do more than briefly examine a few Negro spirituals as illustrations of the Black slave's religious faith and understanding of God's Word. Those who wish to understand this musical form better (and the people who gave it birth) are encouraged to read some of the excellent books which interpret the spirituals in a clear manner.

"People singing a Negro spiritual are often fascinated and puzzled at one and the same time by the words of the songs." That is how one writer describes people's encounter with the Negro spiritual. The Negro spirituals speak of the Black American's understanding of God, Jesus Christ and the Holy Spirit. They touch on themes such as deliverance and liberation ("Didn't my Lord deliver Daniel?", and "Go down Moses"), crucifixion and resurrection ("Were you there when they crucified my Lord?", and "He rose"), joy and praise, to mention only a few. The understanding of each of these themes as expressed in the spirituals has been derived from a biblical text.

Black worship and the Negro spiritual have been accused at times of being too "other-worldly". The Black movement for racial justice in the 60s showed not only that the Black church and Black worship were relevant, but also that the music of the Black slaves was still relevant to issues such as faith, obedience, suffering and liberation. Probably one of the most familiar of the spirituals is "Go down Moses" which is based on the biblical story of God's calling of Moses and the deliverance of the Hebrews from Egyptian slavery.

> Go down Moses, Way down in Egypt's land,
> Tell old Pharaoh, To let my people go.
> When Israel was in Egypt's land, Let my people go!
> Oppressed so hard they could not stand, Let my people go!
> Thus saith the Lord bold Moses said, Let my people go!
> If not I'll smite your first-born dead, Let my people go!
> No more in bondage shall they toil, Let my people go!
> Let them come out with Egypt's spoil, Let my people go!

This spiritual clearly is about God as the deliverer of the Israelites from Egypt — the Exodus. However, it also was a song of consolation and assurance of what God could still do for those who are oppressed. (There is another spiritual about deliverance which says, "Didn't my Lord deliver Daniel, then why not every Man?")

While the inspiration for the text of this spiritual was the biblical account of the Israelites' liberation from Egyptian slavery, the interpretation given in the singing of this song always has a contemporary meaning. For the slaves the Southern USA was Egypt. The slave master was Pharaoh. The Black slaves were the ancient Hebrews. And the deliverer was God working through those who would eliminate slavery. In the 1960s the Moses for many Black Americans would have been Martin Luther King, Jr. Today, Black Christians in the USA cannot sing "Go down Moses" without thinking of oppressed brothers and sisters in South Africa.

If "Go down Moses" is among the most familiar spiritual, one of the best-loved spirituals among Black Americans is "Ev'ry time I feel the Spirit". This song speaks of the reality of the Pentecost and the power of the Holy Spirit:

Ev'ry time I feel the Spirit,
Moving in my heart, I will pray.
Ev'ry time I feel the Spirit,
Moving in my heart, I will pray.
Upon the mountain my Lord spoke
Out of His mouth came fire and smoke.
All around me looked so fine,
Asked my Lord if all was mine.
Jordan river, chilly and cold,
Chills the body but not the soul.

There is in this spiritual knowledge, for example, of the story of the Pentecost when the Spirit was bestowed on the people. It recounts Moses' encounter with God and his receiving of the Law; the transfiguration when the splendour was such that the disciples wanted to build "booths" and remain there forever, and the baptism of Jesus.

It is the presence of the Spirit which would move one to pray. And for the Black people who originated and shaped the spirituals, there is only one Spirit — the Holy Spirit. This theme is further developed in the spiritual which says "I'm going to pray when the Spirit says pray. I'm going to sing when the Spirit says sing. I'm going to shout when the Spirit says shout. And obey the Spirit of the Lord." In other words, whatever the Spirit says, that we will do.

The spiritual became a way in which the Black slaves recalled the biblical stories and events about which they had heard, and related these to their own live situation, their own faith and hope. So while the message of the spirituals was biblical and historical, yet its applicability was contemporary. It was also prophetic for it applies to God's covenant and promise to his people — especially today's oppressed.

In the words of one writer, the spirituals were faith-engendering and life-affirming for the community of believers who created them. They have been such for the community which has preserved them. The spirituals can be something of the same for people today who seek to understand God and his word in their particular situation. However, for the spirituals to become this, they must be learned and sung by the people who are oppressed.

Some suggested resources on the Negro spirituals

The American Negro Songs and Spirituals, ed. by John W. Work, New York, Bonanza Books, 1940.

Negro Folk Music in USA, Harold Courlander, New York, Columbia University Press, 1963.

Negro Spirituals (Wesen und Wandel geistlicher Volkslieder), Christa Dixon, Wuppertal Jugenddienst-Verlag (German and English), 1967. An excellent study of spirituals with biblical text source identified.

Negro Spirituals from Bible to Folksong, Christa K. Dixon, Philadelphia, Fortress Press, 1976.

The Spirituals and the Blues, James H. Cone (an interpretation), New York, Harper & Row, 1972.

Slave Religion, the "Invisible Institution" in the Antebellum South, Albert J. Raboteau, Oxford University Press, 1978.

"Somebody's Calling my Name", Black Sacred Music and Social Change, Wyatt T. Walker, Valley Forge, PA, Judson Press, 1979.

"Lift Every Voice and Sing", a Collection of Afro-American Spirituals and Other Songs, Church Hymnal Corporation, 800 Second Avenue, New York 10017.

The Parable
of the Importunate Widow

MARIA TERESA PORCILE and ANGELICA FERREIRA

The situation

Friday afternoon, 17 October. The farewell meeting for Marie Madeleine also gave us the chance for the two Bible groups to meet together.

We read Luke 18:1-8. The reading was first done aloud and then each person quietly read the passage again.

After the reading we spontaneously told each other which verse had most caught the attention of each member of the group. For many it was the first: "... always to pray and not lose heart" (Esther, Marie Madeleine, Teresita, Traute)... Verse 7 interested Mary and Angelica and also Juanita, Elsa and Susana...

Doña Santa said:

> What strikes me is that she does not lose heart; because I pray to God, but I lose heart...

We considered who the people in the parable are: the judge is a man who has power; the widow is a woman who is poor and humble, perhaps having problems with her neighbours...

Juanita drew our attention to the topical nature of this parable. Angelica said:

> This widow is typical of heaps of people; it is important to see ourselves in this widow; there are times when we unwittingly have this experience...

She went on:

> For instance we saw how those poor children from the slums looked... and when we saw them in the film we realized they were our children. The same thing happens in the story. This is an everyday situation and Jesus tells us about it in a parable and calls our attention to it. It is actually an everyday occurrence and it matters...

Doña Santa picked up this thread:

> Sometimes I ask myself where God is. We talk a lot about God, of course...
> but is our heart where our mouth is? for we cannot lie to God...

Angelica said:

> I think we are always asking and never giving.

Someone else said:

> What matters is to keep at it all the time and to win — not just to try once
> and then be weary of it...

As we continued thinking in silence, Elsa suddenly broke the silence:

> I too think we have to be patient. We asked before and we are still asking
> but everything has its proper occasion. I am beginning to learn not to worry so
> much because everything has its proper moment.

Doña Santa said:

> I was impatient.

Juanita said:

> For me what matters is that the woman insists and the judge gives. You
> have to be strong and keep pushing.

Angelica came in again:

> But really, if you think about it, that judge fellow is not the giver. God is the
> giver. Not "the Father", but God. That's what I think... And it seems to me
> that God has given us hands and feet... Sometimes I think that though in one
> way God has given me nothing, after all he has given me everything. I have
> nothing, yet I have everything. When I'm with my husband and children I
> think I have everything — I have my health and we are all together. And he
> has given me everything because he gave me feelings and the ability to
> sympathize with other people's sorrows...

Juanita interrupted:

> I also think we are vulnerable but at the same time there is a stage in life that
> is completed. I used to think of death as something horrible and I once
> happened to read what Saint Paul says in the letter to the Corinthians about our
> being like a seed, and I understood...

Then Esther, who had been thinking to herself, said:

> Prayer is faith. What this widow had was much faith... The judge kept
> forgetting that someone other than himself was in charge. He was not as

strong as he thought. God was up there and it was God who took care of the widow.

We asked Marie Madeleine for her thoughts (it was the last time she would be with us in this course). She said:

> To me what matters is when God chose to intervene. There is a time and there is a place of God's choosing just as there is a time of waiting which requires patience. And so through patience prayer is purified and becomes less self-centred...
>
> For at times prayer can be a struggle or a contest. What matters is that God always answers. It happens that he does not always answer according to what we want or think or believe; and at times though he answers his answer is "No" or sometimes "Wait". There are different ways of answering.

Esther's comment on this was:

> I think prayer is like a demonstration of faith... there is a gap between the prayer and God's reply... if one grew tired of trying...

We then went back to the text of the Gospel and asked:

> But what kind of story is this in the Gospel? Does it tell of an actual event?

The whole group said: "Yes, it actually happened". We then decided to re-read it carefully to see if it did really tell of an actual event... (we read it over more than once in silence): we noted that in fact it says Jesus was going to tell a parable. So it did not really happen...(?)...

But we all said: O yes, it did, because it is the kind of thing that does happen... We noted that Jesus taught from real life and did not invent strange things. He simply teaches us to interpret events, the things that happen.

On that occasion he gave the example of a widow: in that age she is neglected, unprotected, and with no laws to defend her.

Jesus takes what is most neglected in the society of his day — a woman on her own. We analyzed the text more closely, remembering that Jesus has drawn this example from his society, *his* age, *his* culture and asked: if instead of being in Palestine 2,000 years ago Jesus was here among us how would he tell this parable today? How could we tell it now in our own situation? What is the equivalent of the widow? Who is the unsympathetic judge?...

The smiling, unanimous answer was... the authorities!

This is where the fun started... Will people know the parable? And what if we were to go and read it to the official in charge? We could already see ourselves sitting on the stairs of the local government offices

waiting to read it. The poor have a marvellous sense of humour which is
the product of suffering, detachment and relativity. To this someone said:

> But we must have faith when we go...

We then noted something more serious: we were reading the Gospel
passage which would be read the next Sunday in all the city's churches...
and throughout the world!

Many people with authority in our society (unknown to us: perhaps the
offical in charge himself), many judges who can judge the situation of
"many widows" and many of life's problems... would be listening to that
parable in Sunday services the next day. Many would be Christians, we
thought, and would even know the story... or would they?

It was remarkable to be thinking together about this fact, so simple and
so true: throughout Uruguay and the world and in all the shanty towns the
whole church would be reading this parable to which we were listening
and on which we were meditating. We were thoughtful... It was a very
sobering thought that such a fundamental parable, about which we had
discovered so many things, would be heard next day by so many men and
women, perhaps on radio or television too. Would they reflect on it?
Would it change anything?

In a way our group felt itself the guardian of a secret. There was
something we had been digging out of the parable together in prayer and
meditation... For us it had become something special, an expression of
hope and a reason for hope, faith, and steadfastness in prayer. And that
was something very personal. It could be identified with the cry against
injustice and on behalf of the destitute.

We had almost discovered among ourselves something which gave us
the strength to say that God was on our side — on the side of the widow,
poor and alone, and that this God would give an answer... and now we
discovered that this passage would be read the next day and preached
from in all the churches, and throughout the world... Would there be any
hope of change?

Somebody said:

> I don't know: God is forgotten when power and force are involved.

And Angelica said:

> There are some people who don't believe in anything, not even in themsel-
> ves... How are they going to believe in God?

Meanwhile Juanita had been thinking about this matter of belief in God
and she said:

I believe that having children is in itself love. And if there is love there is no atheism.

But something very special had happened. It was the first day we had met in our two groups together... The previous Wednesday the San Vicente group had met for the first time with Traute. And Traute had chosen this parable (knowing nothing about its being the passage from the lectionary for the next Sunday). As for the San Isidro group, it had not chosen the passage but had only taken it for the relevant Sunday.

We thought it extraordinary and providential that there had been this coincidence between the purpose of the San Isidro group and the choice made by the San Vicente group. And the two groups had reflected together.

As we thought about this, there was some curiosity about why Traute had chosen that parable. Looking at Traute we found her frank, honest and open: she had been very quiet. Of course she still did not understand all the nuances of Spanish, but we had such confidence in her that we thought her able to tell us openly why she had chosen that parable in particular, so we asked her. And she said:

> I really don't know, but I think there were two reasons:
>
> 1) I have been around for three weeks and still don't know much, but from what I can see, it is my belief that women are the leaders, the driving force. And therefore if they are the motive power this parable is meant for you...
>
> 2) The other reason is that this very parable is the last one that I read in the group of women with whom I met in Germany. And there were many parallels in our reflection and we also asked whom that unsympathetic judge with power represents for us today. The answer there was somewhat different because our situation makes it different: we all thought the unsympathetic judge represented those controlling the armaments race and above all nuclear weapons.

Our group was silent and thoughtful. Traute was bringing a problem to our attention which was not directly familiar to our group. Of course we knew about nuclear weapons, missiles etc., but when all was said these were a long distance away... such a long distance. On the other hand, hungry children, diseases, the lack of running water and rats in the houses were all so near at hand, yet everything in our situation that is so sad and squalid seemed so harmless compared to the possibility and immediate threat of worldwide catastrophe — and our reflections became deeper and drifted towards the invisible chains of blind power... and perhaps towards the world's centres of power, invisible and "blind" too.

The group also discovered that in both societies power was exclusively, or for the most part, in the hands of men with decision-making authority and that they had the power of life and death; also that in both societies there were women importunately seeking justice, going into action and creating the feeling for a humane society.

Conclusion of the afternoon

We had discovered the "role" of a poor woman in the gospel and identified her with the women of a slum, marginalized district in Latin America and also with the middle-class women in a developed, industrialized European country. Each in their own environment — and the situation was the same: they were women crying out for a just order. In the two different societies there were two types of women living socially in different situations but they could both be identified with the neglected widow.

It seemed to us that the woman represents importunate faith. She cries out, organizes herself and also struggles against a situation she interprets as powerlessness... she *is importunate:* she does not lose heart.

Something similar happens with the figure of the judge. There's a difference, but in the end it is the same: there are political forces moved by competition, money, the lust for power, insensitivity to the cries and suffering of the underprivileged.

With a national government women feel that the political authorities are insensitive to their situation; but they act, they are on the move, they organize themselves, they cook for the whole slum quarter... they plan festivals, etc.

In international politics women also act, faced with the prospect of a war that may endanger human survival: they get on the move and organize demonstrations.

Closing our meeting with a moment of prayer we noted that theological reflection on this parable must be set against the background of Jesus' purpose: he was teaching about constant prayerfulness: "always to pray and not lose heart". With this parable Jesus tells us how to pray: with faith, hope, persistence, and untiringly, to the limits of our patience...

The women of the South and those of the North, those in the Latin American slums and of the middle-class in the northern hemisphere come together with the one cry and feel that their persistence in their requests will one day give them the strength to overcome those who neither "fear God nor regard man".

The parable does not say that the judge was converted. We don't know about that. The parable indicates the power of the cries of the poor and of prayer as an expression of their faith. Even if the judge does not answer God will respond. There is only one condition: faith and prayer. The final question is:

> Do we have that faith? Do we believe in the efficacy of our cries? Do we place our hope in the power of our complaints?

Two months later

The Bible study about the widow did not stop there. It was developed into something surprisingly fruitful and this is how it happened.

On 31 December at 4 in the afternoon, the chief local official, the president of the Banco Hipotecario and a whole procession of people from the authorities came to the quarter, also some of the wives from what the newspapers call "the governmental hierarchy". There was something different about the slums... an air of expectation and bustle. In the middle of a field which is normally used as a football pitch a large table had been placed with a nylon cloth and in addition a bunch of flowers.

For those of us who knew the everyday appearance of the slums this was an unusual and artificial spectacle. Even the neighbours there seemed to waver between scepticism and hope. A kind of contract was going to be signed with the Banco Hipotecario, involving the building of thirty houses with the participation of the people. It was 31 December. On the one hand the people smelt a whiff of bureaucracy... were there some formalities on which to end the year and be able to say that an agreement had been signed in 1986? Would that be it? Perhaps there was something of that. Nevertheless at the same time a little hope began to stir. The reaction of the women in the Bible study group was unusual:

> Look: there is the town clerk. Why not let us go and read the story of the widow to him?

Two months had gone by since our meeting and we had dealt with other themes... but the widow was still there in the women's hopes.

It was a mischievous question, smilingly asked. I personally knew the town clerk, through family connections. I said: Why not?

When the public event was over we went forward to find and greet him. Suddenly he found himself surrounded by strong, determined, smiling women.

I introduced myself and reminded him who I was. He asked after my family, my father and so on. A brief formal moment of full human relationships. After this initial conversation the group was introduced:

> Mr X... these neighbours have something to say to you.

There were smiling introductions and the women began to speak.

> "And when are we getting the water?"
> "What water?"
> "The water for the emergency houses in which we have been living for thirty years with no water and no windows..."
> "What?" (The town clerk called over the architect, a high official of the state health organization.).

Confusion about details... promises of a quick reply... alarm on 31 December at the prospect of a January that would be passed in the sun on the beach.

The women stressed the urgency and the date. They did the same as Maria Canà had done. Hope was on the march; and in its train came organization and complaints, there were comings and goings between the slums and the state offices. There was an attitude of a just struggle for their rights. Determined resistance to delays, to interminable negotiations and excuses.

And finally the water arrived, in January, the warmest month of the year, and there was a celebration in the slums: a *water celebration*, with buckets and hoses and smiles and colourfulness and singing.

And the women said: "Do you see? The widow's story has come true?"

A year later I asked Angelica if she remembered the incident of the widow. With a full, radiant smile she said:

> With the passage about the widow and the arrival of the water many people who had believed in nothing became aware that if a struggle is carried on justly and with faith everything can be achieved. And today we are convinced that our wealth lies in the fact of our great poverty, since it keeps us united and God is with us.

And I kept thinking that today as yesterday the Lord is still being born in the city slums — in the marginalized suburbs. That is where Emmanuel appears.

Midwives Subvert a Royal Mandate

SHARON RUIZ-DUREMDES and PACITA GARGANERA

The place: A retreat house set in a restful valley surrounded by rolling hills where all one hears are the wind and the birds.

The event: A Bible sharing time with fifteen Filipina women from all walks of life and one American lady observer.

* * *

Facilitator: Listen to that wind — mighty strong, isn't it? What does that remind you of?

Response: Power!

Response: Power? Whose power?

Response: Definitely not ours.

Facilitator: Why not?

Response: I'm not that naive to think we have power as strong as that wind!

Response: But doesn't the Bible say that God gave us power to become the children of God?

Facilitator: Maybe the Bible can show us other things.

Response: The Bible is biased against women. All the great stories are about men! And that tent-maker-trying-hard-to-be-theologian must have been a woman hater!

Facilitator: Is the Bible really biased against us? Does it really set out to deliberately discriminate against us?

Response: It all depends on who is reading the Bible.

Response: Just look at that chapter in Proverbs about the virtuous (said sarcastically) woman! (women turn their Bibles to Proverbs 31:10-31)

Facilitator: That's a good place to start. Let's read it.

Response: I'm just wondering... if the wife does all that, what does her husband do?

Response: Sits beside the city gate and boasts to the elders of the land about his virtuous wife! (laughter)

Response: I think this is so stupid!

Response: Which one? The husband or the virtuous woman? (laughter)

Response: This whole passage! The wife works so hard and it's the husband that is well known in the land!

Response: But at least the husband is "kind" enough to praise her — says verse 29.

Response: But that praise is very oppressive! It's kind of like an anesthetic. That's just what my husband does — praises me so I won't complain, you know!

Response: And look at verse 30! That's the limit. It just legitimizes woman's oppression! What that says to me is: Never mind if you look like an old hag — what is important is that you fear God! After the wife weaves, brings food from out-of-the-way places, prepares meals before daylight, plants a vineyard, sews bedspreads, etc. One doesn't expect her to look charming and beautiful. She doesn't have the time or the energy to fix herself. But that's all right: beauty is fleeting and charm is deceptive! That's all right because there's no one to pretty up for, anyway. Your husband is busy sitting at the city gate talking with the elders! (laughter) Just fear God and don't mind those wrinkles!

Facilitator: Aha! Fear God! What does *fear God* mean, anyway? Let's look at a story in Exodus 1:8-22. Maybe we can discover how "fear of God" must be defined. (all turn their Bibles to the passage. Silence as everyone reads individually)

Response: Wow! Very heavy!

Facilitator: Indeed it is. What does the text tell you?

Response: First, this new king — he is Exhibit Number One for what tyranny is.

Facilitator: How do you know that?

Response: Well, verse 12 clearly says the Egyptians oppressed the Israelites... hard labour!

Response: But you know the king is really a coward. Tyrants are actually cowards. They devise means to make people forget their power... to crush their spirits, the Bible says.

Response: I didn't know there was LIC (Low Intensity Conflict) back in those days! (laughter)

Facilitator: Where do you see that?

Response: Verses 13 and 14? Not only did the Egyptians force the Israelites to work but also impressed them with infrastructure projects and with the abundance of resources from the field! You know in my barrio (village), the government has been busy building roads into out-of-the-way places...

Response: That's for counter-insurgency purposes!

Response: Exactly! And all those buildings coming up! I wonder who they'll put in there.

Response: Don't forget the armoured cars and army trucks that parade up and down the main streets!

Facilitator: A show of force?

Response: No, a desperate attempt to prove to themselves that they are in control but we know better...

Facilitator: Let's go back to our story.

Response: This new king, I think he is a male chauvinist through and through.

Facilitator: Why do you say that?

Response: Because he tells the midwives to exterminate the male babies but to let the girls live.

Facilitator: And so?

Response: And so what he is saying is this: Let the girls live — they are weak, they can't do us harm. But the boys, kill them. They are the ones who will rise up against us some day.

Response: Little does this "macho man" know that it is *women* — two humble, harmless women who subvert his royal mandate!!! (applause)

Facilitator: But why do these midwives disobey the king?

Response: Because they feared God. They were God-fearing.

Facilitator: Now, what does that mean to you? What is "fear", anyway — in the context of our story, that is?

Response: Reverence for God... and life.

Response: It is undivided loyalty. The midwives were loyal only to God and, therefore, they had no qualms about disobeying the king.

Response: To fear God means, for me, doing what I firmly believe is right.

Facilitator: But what or who is your standard for right-ness? For the midwives, what made them believe what they were doing was right?

Response: Their work... their vocation. As midwives, their work was to usher in life — not to destroy it. To help the process of delivery was what they were doing and were trained to do. In the context of that vocation, because they were taking their work very seriously, a sense of rightness emerged.

Response: You mean doing what comes naturally?

Response: Yes, and for a person of faith — that is God's revelation. Haven't you experienced that when you do your work seriously, you don't go about deliberately making wrong decisions? If you do, these are honest mistakes, right?

Facilitator: And so when we say we fear God, what that really means is listening to our own sense of what is right which emerges from doing our work seriously. Am I correct?

Response: Beautifully worded. It's better said than done, though. There's just too many pressures.

Response: And sometimes our sense of rightness can be so distorted. Like for many of my colleagues at the office, they have already internalized the values of the oppressive ruling class that they cannot any more identify with the struggles of the poor. And yet, they, too are being oppressed.

Response: God put you there in that office to conscientize them!

Response: Can we go back to the midwives? I just now received some kind of insight. These humble, harmless midwives were involved in a scheme that had national implications. What they did had some bearing on the life of a nation. It could be something like civil disobedience... and it had nation-wide consequences. What that tells me is that we, women, must change our issues. Instead of the petty, inconsequential, superficial issues we enjoy talking about — fashion, food, the live-in partner of so-and-so — we must be involved in matters affecting the life of our nation.

Response: But those midwives didn't change their issues... their work, that is. They continued to do exactly what they had done before.

Facilitator: I don't see a whole lot of contradiction between the two points. I guess we can put it this way: Let us do our specific tasks or jobs and make them count for the welfare of the country.

Response: But what if you're trafficking drugs?

Response (a peasant woman): Then traffic arms! (Varied reactions.) No, I'm just kidding!

Response: That's still changing the issue!

Facilitator: By the way, what can Donna say? (referring to the American woman who was an observer in the Bible sharing)

Response: She has changed her issue! That's why she has come to the Philippines!

Donna: Yes, I've followed your discussion with great interest. I feel it's very exciting the way you read the Bible. The women back home have a lot to learn from you all. It's so inspiring...

Response: But that inspiration should lead you into some action!

Donna: Right! Since I've been here, I've really been asking myself what I could do when I return to be in solidarity with your struggles here. I could raise money to...

Response: Don't reduce our struggle to a mere fund-raising campaign. Filipinos do not live by bread alone...

Response: Filipinos don't live, period! What with all the misery and oppression!

Facilitator: I guess Donna means something entirely different.

Response: Yes, I understand. Perhaps solidarity can take different forms. For instance, people in Nicaragua and El Salvador should continue to wage their struggle against foreign intervention for their victory is also our victory. In like manner, we also should persevere in our own struggle here in the Philippines.

Response: Or Donna can help educate her own people on the relationship between her country's policies and our misery. She can tell her friends that when her country sneezes, we, Filipinos catch a cold!

Response: Or in countries that have successfully thrown off the yoke of foreign domination and begun the process of reconstruction, they need to make their model so attractive and commit themselves to making it work so that those of us who are yet waging our struggle against foreign domination may learn from them.

Response: But we are no longer talking about the Bible.

Facilitator: We have changed our issue?

Response: No, not exactly. We are doing just what the midwives did — listening to our own sense of what is right and looking for ways of concretizing it.

Facilitator: That is our way of fearing God, isn't it?

Who Will be the Godparents at our Child's Baptism?

MARTIN CORDES and MEMBERS
OF SCHOOL CHAPLAINCY GROUP, HANOVER

This is part of a drama on "Being a Christian in the Established Church", presented at the WCC Central Committee meeting, Hanover, August 1988.

Actors: Secretary, Pastor Krüger, Deaconess Weise-Fischer, the Dreyers
Set: Office with typewriter and personal computer, files.
Study of the pastor, desk, chairs, etc.

Part 1

The secretary is sitting at the desk, working at the personal computer. Suddenly there is a bleep — the computer is defective.

The Dreyers enter. The husband pushes the pram. The secretary is nervous because of the PC, and seems to be frantic.

Mr Dreyer: Let me see! (He goes to the PC, presses the right button, the defect is corrected.) Sheer brilliance!

Secretary: Fantastic, how you managed to do that!

* * *

Secretary: What can I do for you?

Mrs Dreyer: We'd like to have our child baptized.

Secretary: Yes, all right. Have you got your legal documents and the child's birth certificate? And oh, what about the papers of the godparents?

Mrs Dreyer: (shakes her head) No, we haven't, we didn't know about that.

Secretary: Well, then let me have your name and address first.

Mrs Dreyer: (somewhat intimidated) Dreyer, Mauerstrasse 8.

Secretary: (enters the dates into the computer... checks, waits, the text is to be seen on the screen) All right, there it is: Inge Dreyer... (turns to the husband) But you are not registered here?

Mr Dreyer: I am not a member of the church. I can believe in God without the church.

Secretary: Let me take down your particulars, you will have to speak with the pastor anyhow. Let me see... Dreyer, Mauerstrasse 8... Do you remember the date of your marriage?

Mrs Dreyer: (abashed) We only had a civil wedding.

Pastor enters the office.

Secretary: I think it's best for you to speak to the pastor right now. (makes a gesture to Pastor Krüger)

Pastor: Good morning. What can I do for you?

Secretary: These are Mr and Mrs Dreyer. They want their child to be baptized.

Pastor: Oh I see. (turns to the Dreyers) If you have time, you may come in right now. (gesture to the study, all of them enter)

Part 2

(The Dreyers squeeze into the sofa and quite evidently feel uneasy. The pram is allowed to be pushed into the study.)

Pastor: (looks into the pram) Is this your first child? How old is he?

Mrs Dreyer: 16 weeks... (hesitatingly) but he causes a lot of trouble already.

Pastor: Oh, does he?

Mrs Dreyer: Yes, shortly after his birth he came out in a rash, and since then our child needs regular medical treatment — we have to be very careful about his food —- but we do not know anything definite yet...

Pastor: That's not too easy for you then, I'm afraid.

Pastor: (jovially) Well, let's come to the point. You want your child to be baptized, right? (pause — at a loss)

Mrs Dreyer: Oh well,... we thought... (hesitates) It's a good thing to have our child baptized ... we have been looking forward to having this baby so much... my husband was even with me during birth. It seems to be a miracle, you know... and we were ever so happy when we had seen him.

Pastor: And now you want to ask God for his blessing in the baptism. That's a good thing. What's the name of your child?

Mrs Dreyer: Christian... My mother also tells us: the child musn't grow up as a heathen.

Mr Dreyer: (almost interrupts) What do we have to do during the baptism? I have never been to a christening!

Pastor: Well, I shall be reading Jesus' words: "Go forth therefore and make all nations my disciples; baptize men everywhere in the name of the Father and the Son and Holy Spirit." Then your child will be blessed by the sign of the cross. And then the parents and the godparents will be asked: "Do you want your child to be baptized?" And only when you answer: "Yes, with the help of God" can I baptize your child.

Mr Dreyer: Do we have to say the creed? Individually? (scared and embarrassed)

Pastor: No, no, I shall say it with you... but actually that's your task, it's you who represents your child, since he is not able to profess the faith for himself.

(The Dreyers look at each other in embarrassment)

And you will have to promise to bring up your child in the Christian faith. The godparents will have to promise that too... Have you already chosen the godparents? They must be ready, after all, to take over this task of Christian education.

Mr Dreyer: We haven't come to a final decision yet. I have been thinking of a colleague of mine... we get along quite well... he plays very kindly with our Christian...

Pastor: Well, you may think about that. Just ring me up when you have decided on the date, and let me know of the names of the godparents, then.

Mr Dreyer: (gets up with a sigh of relief) Well... well... that's that... We'll keep in touch...

Pastor: Perhaps we'll see each other some time in church: I would be pleased.

Mr Dreyer: Yes, yes...

The Dreyers say good bye and push the pram towards the door. Mr Dreyer wipes his face with a handkerchief and shows signs of relief...

Pastor: Good bye...

Part 3

The deaconess enters the office. She meets the Dreyers who are about to leave.

Good bye.

Deaconess: Who were they?

Secretary: That was the Dreyer family. They want their child to be baptized.

Pastor: (turns to the deaconess) Oh, you are here already;... I must apologize, I've just had a talk on baptism.

(turns to the secretary) Mrs Blaue, I am dying for a cup of coffee... would you be so kind?

Pastor and deaconess go to the study.

Pastor sinks into the sofa and takes a deep breath...

Deaconess: Any difficulties?

Pastor: How would you explain baptism to somebody who has no idea about it whatsoever?

Deaconess: Those two want you to baptize their child? Quite a good thing to have that wish, isn't it. After all, it's a good sign. There seems to be some sort of relationship to the church at least... Mind you, I think it would be better for the parents to wait until their child can decide for himself whether he wants to be baptized or not. A friend and I attended a baptismal service in a free church the other day. All the candidates were over 14, and before being baptized each one had to explain in his own words why he wanted to be christened. It was a very personal sort of confession.

Pastor: But... we have in common with the Baptists and other free churches practising believers' baptism faith in Jesus Christ and its witness in this world. We won't renege on what we have in common, even though we haven't reached agreement on the question of baptism.

Deaconess: Still, if someone consciously decides in favour of his baptism — he actually lives with his baptism. I shan't have my children baptized as babies.

Pastor: If that happened, I'd like a word with you as your superior.

Deaconess: But practising infant baptism yourself, you must come to see how little people think about the meaning of baptism. What counts to them is nothing but the celebration of their child's happy birth in church and their wish for a guardian angel.

Pastor: (coffee) I am concerned about the stand you are taking on believers' baptism. After all, baptism is a gift from God — you can't work for it yourself! In baptism I'm given the promise of God's grace — and this cannot be obtained by achievement, as it is well known... God's grace is given to me... "without my achievement"...

Deaconess: Perhaps it's the automatic membership of the church by infant baptism that bothers me. And then, it's only logical that people leave the church. There were 53 of them in our congregation last year. I can't help thinking the desire to baptize infants only produces faithful church tax payers. Infant baptism in order to keep up the established church — you don't want to dig your own grave. Wouldn't it be better to postpone baptism until people want to be faithful members of the church? What matters to me is the question of what will become of baptism afterwards...

Pastor: And what matters to me is the question of what baptism *gives* us. It's the little child who has nothing, who is empty-handed, and God accepts him the way he is.

Deaconess: Quite right — and later on there is the confirmation —

Pastor: (continues his explanation) ... or just think of the original meaning of "sin" which means isolation. Many people are ill, because we set up an artificial world between the creator and creation. Aren't small children manipulated already, remote-controlled? In baptism we encourage parents not to lose sight of the relationship to God.

Deaconess: Nevertheless I'm in favour of believers' baptism. That's simply more honest. I know why I have been baptized and I can remember it!

Pastor: That's a good cue: to remember baptism. Look here! (he reaches to the book shelf) That's what one of my fellow-clergymen presented in the pastors' conference the other day: a candlestick in remembrance of baptism. Quite a good idea! At the age of five the baptized children are invited to the service and each child is given a candlestick like this. Then we practise a song. Wait a minute... you will know that too. It goes like this: (At first the pastor hums, then the group sings and the audience joins in:)

Canon: "I will thank you, for you know my name, Lord of my life."

Part 4

Inge: Erich, the news starts!

Erich: I come, I come...

Inge: Tell me, how is it that you are thinking of Karl as god-father?

Erich: Don't you like Karl? He is a nice chap, I really like him. Of course we need someone else, too. What about your father?

Inge: I wonder if he would do it?

Erich: Hm... he is not even a member of the church...

Inge: I have been thinking of my cousin...

(break)

Inge: But your job is safe...?

Erich: Of course, certainly...

Erich: I hope the weather is fine at Christian's baptism, so that we can go outside...
(The couple has fallen asleep in front of the TV after having shortly discussed during the news who should be considered as a godfather/ godmother.)

Dream
I ask you, are you ready to be this child's godfather and to contribute to his Christian education?

Grandfather: *Of course,* I am. After all I have tried all my *life* to be a good Christian. Christianity is more or less the basis of our culture. I am not a churchgoer, it's true, but I've always believed *in God*. When I'm in the open country and think about the world I have a deep *religious feeling* and *know* that there must be a God.

And then, our pastor knows his job quite well. As I said before, I don't attend church, but from what my wife says, it sounds quite good. He does not interfere with everyday politics. He really takes care of the *souls* in his parish. Maybe, I will attend church some day...

Thus I ask you, are you ready...

Of course I am — that's to say: if my daughter asked me right now, whether I'd like to be this child's godfather — I'd feel uneasy about it. I did say so once, but will she remember?

I left church in those days, you know. You must *understand* that. I worked with the railways of the Reich then as an electrician, I had a promising job. You had to be a member of the Party, at least formally. I never backed Hitler. But still — you must admit — round about 1936/37 everything seemed to be quite all right. Economy began to flourish, there was no unemployment. That *was something* at least. Hitler is said to have killed 6.5 million Jews — until 1945 I had never heard a word about it. Maybe some hints... but I didn't set great store by them.

When the war broke out, oh yes, I somehow felt, that it was bound to go *wrong*. Hitler was a megalomaniac. Well..., but before? It was more or less a matter of good form to leave church. This didn't do any harm to my faith. Actually, after the war I wanted to go back to the church, but then I got *angry* that the church declared *all of us guilty* for what happened during the Third Reich. To me, at least, that does not apply.

Well, that's why I did not join the church immediately after the war — although my wife would have liked me to. And later? I simply forgot about it — reconstruction, etc., you know? There was practically no time left. Some time ago I told my children. But if my daughter asked me today? I could join the church now, but I'd feel embarrassed.

In short, baptism is the right thing. Fundamentally, I'm in favour of it. A child should know right from the beginning where he belongs to.

Are you ready to be this child's godfather and to contribute to his Christian education?

Well, *I* am in favour of it *all*. But they should find a younger godfather, they've such a lot of good friends. Or else — my wife! That would be a good idea. She knows much more about these things! And *I* would have the *opportunity* of attending church, right oh.

Are you ready to be this child's godmother and to contribute to his Christian education?

Cousin: How I'd like to do that! I've already prayed that my cousin would have Christian baptized, so that he might be taken up into the fellowship of Jesus. If only her husband knew what it means to believe in Jesus Christ! — Otherwise I have no hope whatsover — there is too much evil around us... and all those mistakes of ours which we make again and again.

The most important thing for us is to find forgiveness in our group and to serve Jesus Christ in our lives. Since we all have different jobs, there are always new experiences which we share with each other. When we are together in the group, we can speak about everything. The Bible reassures us again and again that faith in Jesus Christ opens our eyes to many things.

Are you ready...

Oh yes, and I'd like to take over the Catholic tradition of a candlestick and take him one for his baptism. For there are also some Catholics in our group. Baptism is something we have in common, and now even the exact wording of the creed, the Lord's Prayer and the common ecumenical translation of the Bible. That's fantastic! In Lent we Protestants have even thought of a kind of fasting. Each one does without a favourite habit, such as sweets, alcohol and cigarettes and gives money for "Bread for the World".

And to contribute to his Christian education?

Yes, yes; and I will think carefully about what I could give Christian for his confirmation. When I was confirmed it was quite terrible. Most of us were given a stereo unit or about 1,500 marks in cash. Today the youngsters of 13 or 14 long for a computer — if they don't have one already — or else want money for their driver's licence. I myself was very happy to receive a hymn book and a two volume history of arts. I still like to look through it today. Well, with all my heart: Yes!

I ask, are you ready to be this child's godfather and to contribute to his Christian education?

Friend: Well, but that's a question of conscience! How on earth did they think of me? Perhaps because I spoke positively about the church some day? And I stick to what I've said. For all the church does in the field of youth unemployment — good for them! Our trade unions could take a leaf out of their book. You may say that is used as an alibi, the church gives us the impression that something is done for the unemployed. That is not the *solution* of the whole problem, quite true, but still, something is being done at least.

All the same, I am not a faithful churchgoer. I'm a guy who likes to see to it that something is done in the end. As to that the church comes off quite well. And there is the question of the handicapped or the old people — or else the persons seeking asylum. In this field the church is really outspoken. And then, these peace initiatives and third-world groups — there is a hell of a lot going on in the church.

But as to what the pastors say in Sunday services and what we were to learn by heart in confirmation classes — that was no use to me when I was young.

I ask you...

Just a moment. Sometimes I had thought about leaving the church because I reject its dogma. The creed, at least, I can't say. Virgin Birth, resurrection and the Last Judgment — I don't believe in. Therefore —

On the other hand, the work of the church has to be financed somehow.

If Erich asked me whether I'd like to be Christian's godfather — I'd say yes.

I do respect anybody's decision. Therefore we did not have our daughter baptized. We wanted her to decide for herself at a later time. And now fancy: the other day we enrolled her at school and were asked about her denomination. I told them Maike has not been baptized, that means — no denomination. But she is meant to attend Protestant religious lessons.

At home Maike said: Why didn't you have me baptized? I want to be christened when I go to school. I believe in God and in heaven where Granny is now.

I ask you...

Well, if Erich asked me — I'd say yes.

Contributors

The Rev. Dr Don Carrington is presently director of the Uniting Church Institute for Mission. He was formerly on the faculty of Nungalinya College, a training centre for Aboriginal leaders in Australia.

The Rev. Johnathon Hogarth is a graduate student who participated (and recorded the experience) in the workshop that produced the material in the article.

Ms Jane Haapiseva (Canada) is the animator of a house Bible study group at La Rippe (near Geneva, Switzerland) and has completed theological studies in Brussels (Belgium) and Geneva.

Ms Jenny Berlie runs the family dairy farm at La Rippe (near Geneva, Switzerland) with her husband. She spent much of her childhood in Turkey.

The Rev. Selvanayagam Israel is a theological teacher at Tamilnadu Theological Seminary in Madurai, India, currently doing doctoral studies in Cambridge, England.

Ms Esther Retnaraj is a member of the women's fellowship of the parish of Zumpropuram, Madurai, India.

The Rev. Francine Carrillo is co-director of the Ecumenical Theological Workshop (AOT), and a pastor in the National Protestant Church of Geneva, Switzerland.

Ms Françoise Larderaz is a Catholic theologian, working part time as a chaplain at a prison in Geneva, Switzerland.

The Rev. Dr Brian B. Haymes is principal of the Northern Baptist College, Manchester, England.

The Rev. Peter Amos is a school teacher turned minister, at the Mount Zion Baptist Church, Lancashire, England.

Mr James M'Namie is a self-supporting evangelist at Mpamba, in the northern region of Malawi.

The Rev. G. Rodney Hodgins is principal tutor of theological education by extension (TEEM) in Malawi.

Dr Ian M. Fraser is research consultant to the Resources Centre for Basic Communities of the Scottish Churches Council.

The Rev. Dr Jaci Maraschin is a priest of the Episcopal Church in Brazil and a professor of hermeneutics at the Ecumenical Programme of Post-Graduate Studies, Sao Paulo, Brazil.

Mr Klécio dos Santos is a leader of the youth movement and a student of journalism in the Catholic University of Pelotas, Brazil.

The Rev. Dr J. Oscar McCloud is the executive director of the Fund for Theological Education (FTE), New York, and a member of the Executive Committee of the World Council of Churches.

Ms Maria Teresa Porcile is a theologian of the Roman Catholic Church in Uruguay. She is preparing a doctorate at the University of Fribourg, Switzerland.

Ms Angelica Ferreira is a member of the San Isidro group (Uruguay) working for social change in the slums.

Ms Sharon Rose Joy Ruiz-Duremdes is regional coordinator of the Western Visayas Ecumenical Council in Iloilo City, Philippines.

Ms Pacita Garganera is a member of the Bible study group in Iloilo City, Philippines.

Dr Martin Cordes is a pastor, coordinator of a group of chaplains and teachers of religion in schools, and of an ad hoc group of dramatists in Hanover, Federal Republic of Germany.

• Creates a picture or an image in the childs mind